Eschatology

A Participatory Study Guide

Edward W. H. Vick

Energion Publications
Gonzalez, FL
October, 2012

Copyright © 2012, Edward W. H. Vick

Scripture quotations marked RSV are from the Revised Standard Version, Copyright © by Division of Christian Education of the National Council of the Churches of Chlst in the United States of America, 1946, 1952, 1971. All other Scripture references are the author's translation.

Cover Design: Henry E. Neufeld

ISBN10: 1-938434-10-2
ISBN13: 978-1-938434-10-5
Library of Congress Control Number: 2012949738

Praise for *Eschatology: A Participatory Study Guide*

In this scholarly and immensely practical work, Dr. Vick walks the participant through a complex theological history. He does so with great clarity and by using examples that will provide material for further study and discussion. His work succeeds at offering both a thorough academic background and a framework for deeper exploration. This work is a valuable contribution to the important and often overlooked field of Adult Christian Education.

Rev. Dr. Robert R. LaRochelle
United Church of Christ Pastor
Author, *Crossing the Street, Part Time Pastor, Full Time Church, So Much Older Then* (forthcoming)

Edward Vick has written a brief yet surprisingly detailed survey of the vast and complicated field of Christian eschatology. One of the greatest contributions that Vick makes is providing operational definitions for many difficult theological concepts, opening up the entire subject to lay and novice readers. In a time captivated by the ending of the Mayan calendar, upcoming catastrophes of cataclysmic proportions, placing the return of the Lord in our day planners, and reading newspaper headlines as Bible prophecy, this book provides a helpful corrective and foundation for a subject that has become untethered from the Bible, theology, and reality.

Rev. Dr. Geoffrey Lentz
United Methodist Pastor
Author, *Learning and Living Scripture, The Gospel According to St. Luke: A Participatory Study Guide, A Living Psalter* (editor)

Table of Contents

1	Foreword	1
2	They Remembered Him	11
3	New Testament Eschatology	19
4	Prophecy And Apocalyptic	27
5	Eschatology And The Quest	43
6	Eschatology Future And Present	51
7	Resurrection	69
8	Words And Meanings	77
9	When 'Jesus Is Coming Again Soon' Cannot Be False	89
	Appendix To Chapter 9	100
10	The End After the End	115
	Bibliography	129

The Participatory Study Series

The Participatory Study Series from Energion Publications is designed around the motto "scholarship in service." Each guide is written by someone with a strong background in the topic studied and designed for use by lay people in Sunday School classes and small groups, as well as for individual study.

These guides are not all easy reading. Some of the topics covered require serious effort on the part of the student. But the guides do provide all the resources necessary for a fruitful study.

The section "Using this Book" is designed for the series but adapted to the particular study guide. Each author is free to emphasize different resources in the study, and to follow his or her own plan in presenting the material.

It is our prayer at Energion Publications that each study guide will lead you to a deeper understanding of your Christian faith.

– Henry Neufeld, General Editor

Using This Book

This study guide is will be found very helpful for small groups, such as Sunday School classes. Individual students working on their own will benefit from the stimulation it provides. It might serve as an introductory textbook.

The book itself will give you with an overview of a topic, Eschatology, providing specific questions for discussion. There are several things you can do to make your study more profitable.

(1) Where **resources** are suggested, divide them between members of the class and consult them during your study time. Students can bring what they have learned to the class. This is also a good time to help your church improve its library. Suggest some of these resources for your library shelves.

(2) **Share.** The Participatory Study Guides to Bible books pioneered sharing as an integral part of your study, but it will work just as well when you are studying a topic. Sharing does not mean harassing other people with your viewpoint. It's a matter of listening and being accountable in your community. If you come to a conclusion, listen to others who can comment on it and possibly point out reasons that you may be wrong, or ideas that may not have occurred to you.

This is the first topical study guide in the series. Eschatology is a complex topic, and there is much misinformation on it in various churches. This guide will provide you with a foundation to understand other discussions and to discern the difficulties with many end-time schemes that you may see presented in popular books and on TV, or held by different churches

1

Foreword

This book provides an introduction to a topic of much interest and importance both in the life of the ordinary believer and in theological circles. For from the very beginning of its existence, the church and every Christian church throughout the history of Christianity has put the topic of the end as an important item in its creed and in the consciousness of the believer.

Today we find very different approaches to the subject of eschatology. It seems strange, as has been noted by many fundamentalist and critical Christians as well as theologians, that eschatology has developed the way it has, so that theologians can talk about the end being realised in the present. How can the 'end' be present? Firmly and insistently most Christians have seen the end as the subject of hope for a consummation in the future, supernaturally introduced as the fulfilment of God's creative act and the transformation of all life as we now know it. Many Christians hold that the Advent of the Christ is to take place speedily and speak of the imminence of the Advent. Some of these have ventured boldly to suggest an actual date, or to set a limit to the intervening years. But not all. Most have been content to confess belief in the consummation and the life everlasting. Others wish to retain the urgency associated with expectation of an immediate, or imminent Advent, but have been adamant that no date can be set, nor can any limit be given to how long we may have to wait before the Advent. What then could they mean by speaking of the Advent as 'soon'?

Christian faith is related to and dependent upon the inheritance from the past. That inheritance goes back to the original witness of the apostles, their disciples, and the church which they served. Their witness is about Jesus who became the Christ. So we may make a distinction between the Aramaic speaking Jesus of Nazareth, Galilee and Jerusalem, and the Christ of the devoted earliest Christians, most of whom lived in the world outside Palestine and who spoke Greek. That witness is contained in the New Testament writings which are, both historically and as revelatory, primary for understanding Jesus Christ. They are both historical documents and also instruments of revelation. As proclamation of the faith, and instruments for the emergence of new faith, they have come to be called *kerygma*.

To account for the inheritance from the past we are reliant upon the results we obtain when we ask questions about the history, both of the documents and of the central figure of the *kerygma*, the proclamation, namely Jesus. The result of such questioning has given rise to a different approach to eschatology from the traditional and conservative one. We shall clarify this. It is also appropriate that a statement making clear what the conservative Christian says about the Advent and the End time be included in an introductory writing on eschatology.

The aim of the writing is to provide a readable introduction to the theme and, by suggesting literature for further reading, to enable readers to build on what is here written should they wish to pursue the topic. Anyone who reads the book seriously will have questions to answer.

Methods of Procedure

How shall we talk about our subject? As a preliminary we shall consider methods of procedure. After all, we ought to know how we are going to answer the question: 'How may we talk profitably about the end time?' There are various approaches to our question. The first four we mention are closely tied to the interpretation of texts taken to be authoritative. Others are the result of systematic, careful thought about the issues that need to be taken into account, but which often do not occur in conservative approaches to the Bible. The issues they raise are of fundamental importance.

(1) The approach of the fundamentalist is to go to the Bible and gather as many texts as refer to the End-time. It is not of primary importance to this 'collect and gather', 'here a little, there a little' approach to inquire when and why the passages were written. All the writings of Scripture are on a level, in terms of authority, and as sources of doctrine. No distinction is made with regard to background or situation. They are not treated historically. The Bible is regarded as a storehouse of truth or truths waiting to be gathered and collated. From this storehouse one can take whatever one sees relevant, from wherever one selects and create from such 'proof texts' an ensemble, now presented as doctrine, as 'the truth.' What is important is to produce a consensus culled from the total collection. It is as if the source was a big box containing many items, set in different packages. It does not matter when, by whom, or for what purpose the packages were put in. Once the box is open you find what you think appropriate, wherever it is in the box. You do not differentiate one source from another. You find and excerpt what you consider appropriate for the construction of a doctrine.

(2) Another method is to focus on a particular writer and study that writer in depth, taking background and assumptions into consideration: for example, the *Gospel of John*, with both its insistence that eternal life is present and with clear references to the resurrection at the last day.[1]

(3) This careful contextual study is then repeated with several writers, or several writings of the same author and the differences between their teaching compared and assessed.

---

1   On *John* 5:29, C. K. Barrett comments: 'They rise to share in the life to come, the *zoe aionios* [eternal life] which those who believe already enjoy (v. 24).' *The Gospel According to St. John*, p. 219.

Paul, in the two books to the Thessalonians for example, writes with enthusiastic anticipation on the one hand and cautious reservation on the other. (*I Thessalonians* 4:15-18, *II Thessalonians* 2:1-5)

(4) A further consideration is the nature and content of prophetic and apocalyptic writings. These set very sharply the problem of interpreting symbolism. They also present the problem of authorship and so of dating. Here what is important is to assess the claim that they are through and through prophetic, in the literal sense of foretelling future events.

(5) A very obvious approach for many committed Christians is to start, expound and end with the positions accepted by their particular religious community, the particular denomination, to which they belong. It is often enough for many in this category simply to accept the teaching of their church and assert it as the decisive and final word. The question to ask is quite simply, 'What do we teach?' Having learned that, or simply knowing what that teaching is, marks the limit of interest in further inquiry. If we have the truth, what further inquiry is needed or even permitted? But one can always ask, 'How did the community come to these positions?' So the conclusions confessed by the community can now be critically examined. How did the 'elders' come to these positions? To what extent did our forebears simply accept what was handed down to them? Can we speak of an original set of beliefs? Then the way lies open to examine the question of the validity of the methods used, and to add, for good measure, the matter of the authority of the teachings.

What is important to consider is that the topic of the End-time, of eternity, resurrection and judgement which is the content of eschatology, is open to a wide range of interests. The simple believer, the creed-maker, and the sophisticated scholar all have an interest in the topic. So there is discussion and assertion on very different levels. Sometimes this gives rise to conflict and antagonism. 'What's the point of such erudite discussion?' asks the simple believer. 'We have hope based on our faith and that is what is satisfactory. Just leave it at that.' 'You must consider what is obvious to any rational person today if you want an acceptable i.e. reasonable understanding' rejoins the other. 'We shall not take the risk of doubt and confusion' says the one. 'If you are not prepared to entertain doubt and find a settlement beyond the doubt, you will remain for ever immature and irrational' says the other.

What should be clear is that it is not only the scholars that disagree. Often there are intense disagreements between simple believers. And conservative theology can become complex. The scholar welcomes such disagreement when it is a means to progress. He is not interested in dogmatism.

(6) Taking account of the understanding of the world we now accept as given, we ask questions that would not and could not have occurred to biblical writers. Such questions are not accepted as basic to fundamentalist interpreters. Since our world-view is so different from ancient, first century and medieval understandings, we have to ask, 'What difference does it make to our assessment of the convictions expressed within the context of that world-view we now have superseded?' 'How may we understand in our context what they understood and expressed in theirs?'

(7) Much writing and discussion has taken place in the last two centuries about the historical Jesus and the importance

of what has come to be called 'eschatology.'[1] The serious systematic and biblical theologian cannot overlook such work, but must consider with all seriousness the questions asked and the answers given. Without such consideration one is not qualified to speak with conviction about the 'End-time'. So an important approach is expressed in the question: 'How does what we know about Jesus immerse us in the theme of eschatology?'

(8) Such approaches assume the importance, and indeed the inevitability, of ready acceptance of the two great revolutions in science and in history. We must study the historical provenance of the scriptural writings, and the evidence for how the documents to which we appeal were constructed. To accomplish this there are well-established principles of historical research. This has particular relevance to our topic. We mention two points. Pseudonymity is well established as an accepted device of ancient writers. This means that in some documents the author attributed to a particular writing is not the actual author. So the dating of the writing is not to be settled by assuming that the author associated with the writing is the actual author. Apocalyptic writers used this device to give authority to their writing, since the figure they associated with their writing was one well known by and having weight with the readers. Since he lived long before the time of the writing or compilation, he had come to be revered in the community. This attribution suggested foreknowledge. That strengthened confidence in the apparent predictions.

(9) The answer we give to the question, 'What difference does it make that you can give an approximate date to the documents of the New Testament?' is that it lets us

---

1 The term 'eschatology' is a modern one. The *Oxford English Dictionary* cites its first use in 1844.

reconstruct the story of the emergence of the church, the Christian community, but only to a certain extent. The fact is that by and large the earliest Christian community had no Christian writings until well past the mid century. By that time it was evident that the Advent, the *parousia*, had not taken place as believers had expected. Anticipations of the imminence of the Second Advent were already outdated. The end had not come.

(10) The earliest Christians had no New Testament. Some of them had the opportunity to hear of a letter from an apostle or from the disciple of an apostle. Others knew of writings and collections presenting the sayings of Jesus. Agreed teachings and structures of authority would emerge later, often much later, when it was clear that the *parousia* was not imminent and so not to be anticipated, even if hope for the Coming and the *eschaton* remained. But there were eye witnesses to the events of Jesus' life and death and their accounts were passed on orally and received in many places as churches emerged throughout the Roman empire. Christian writings came into being as compilations were made and Gospels emerged.

(11) In most of our thinking we take for granted an outlook or 'worldview.' We take a settled attitude to events and causes. We often define the possible in terms of the repeatable. So we try to see if we are able to investigate the causes of unexpected events. We sometimes explain them by successfully probing for their causes. What puzzles us is the occurrence of the non-repeatable counter instance. What baffles us is that we sometimes do not find an explanation of it. We are sometimes not able to state the cause of the phenomenon in question. The fact is that we know much more about the causes of some phenomena than we do of others. But we think we know

that certain kinds of purported, even reported, events just do not happen.

A minimal description of miracle might be in terms of 'non-repeatable counter instance.' But this description would fit other phenomena beside miracles. Repeatableness is important. It is important to be able to find repeated instances of the kind of phenomenon being considered. Observations can then be compared, and evidence gathered and assessed. The principle works like this. If we can find out what the conditions are for producing a particular effect or particular kind of effect we have experienced, we may then go on to produce them and hope to get the anticipated result. This is based on our conviction of the regularity of nature. So we ask, 'What are the necessary and sufficient conditions for producing this effect?' Then we attempt to observe or in the case of experiment to produce these conditions. We then expect and are sometimes rewarded with the same effect. It is this expectation that sustains us in coping with life, and is anticipated in scientific research. If the expected result does not occur, we re-examine the proposal we are making about the set of conditions. In this way we make progress toward knowledge.

No event is causeless. There is no event that is not an effect. When we apply this principle to the task of the historical evaluation of testimony and reports, we shall find that it excludes certain kinds of claims, for example, reports of events the kind of which we do not experience and have not experienced. We disallow such interpretations and may then go on to ask, 'Why did the purported testimony include such events? What did the writer have in mind, and what would his readers understand by his writing?'

A bag of buns does not feed five thousand people, let alone produce twelve baskets of leftovers. What a different world we would live in if, given the right causes, bread and fish multiplied by the hundredfold. We could imagine contests where children with bags of food would compete to see who could feed the most people and who could produce the greatest amount of surplus.

Eschatology

Keep an accurate tally there, how many people Sue has fed! Weigh Johnny's group's leftovers to the ounce! Not our world! Indeed never our world!

So you might ask a few preliminary questions before going on to read this writing. Then you might hold your former answers in abeyance while asking these questions. If you are able to do this frankly and without prejudice, i.e. without letting the answers you would like to give intrude, you will be ready to understand our discussion.

(1) What does the word 'resurrection' mean ?

(2) Since the earth is not flat, what could ascension mean?

(3) How can we distinguish literal from symbolic? If the literal is expressed by the symbolic, what guarantee does one have that one has interpreted the symbol correctly? What is the function of the symbolic?

The answer we give to this question is of particular interest when considering apocalyptic writings, expressing eschatological themes as they do.

(4) Do we apply that same attitude and the same criteria to the texts of Scripture that we accept and use without question in our ordinary dealings and when assessing evidence? We all and always accept the validity of the historical method and of the empirical, or scientific method when assessing reports and making our judgements about events.

(5) What are we to make of assertions that the end is to be speedy when after two millennia the event has not taken place? What meaning shall we give to the various ways of expressing the conviction that the Second Advent is imminent? Shall we say that it is a case of expressing urgency in terms of imminence? What follows from that?

Discussion Questions
Chapter 1

(1) When we read the Bible we are studying historical documents. Is it important to know something about their history and their context?

(2) When interpreting Scripture, what principles is it important to recognise and apply? What approaches should be avoided?

(3) List ways in which our outlook, our world view, differs from that of the ancients or the medievals.

(4) For the early church, the advent did not take place, but the hope persisted. Consider this: Do you find a contemporary parallel?

(5) How do you distinguish between the literal and the symbolic?

(6) Since the advent has not taken place after two thousand years why does the Christian still hope? What does it mean to say that it is 'soon'?

2

THEY REMEMBERED HIM

Jesus' followers remembered him for what he did, for what he said, for what happened to him, and for what they believed him to be. Nor was his scandalous death an ultimate barrier to their faith.

They Might Have Forgotten

However, the records suggest that at one point they might have forgotten — during the interval between Jesus' death and resurrection. It was the interim that they did not recognize as an interim, the period when they judged that Jesus' death meant the end.

Since their hopes had been raised for the fulfilment of all that they and their people had wished for, what better consolation could they enjoy but to forget the whole thing, if they could? The forlorn wail of those whose hopes had been dashed by Jesus' death was, 'But we had hoped that he was the one to redeem Israel. Yes, and besides all this, it is now the third day since this happened' (*Luke* 24:21, RSV). 'Simon Peter said to them, "I am going fishing"' (*John* 21:3). But how could the disciples forget, when they had become a part of what had happened? Perhaps in their despair they could still hope that something else might happen.

Something more did happen. They did not forget. They remembered. The resurrection of Jesus was a turning point. In their Resurrection-faith they came to see that God had not abandoned Jesus in death and that God was even then acting through their very faith. They remembered what he had been because they now knew him for what was happening to them. Jesus was in their midst. When he was spoken about, people experienced and believed. That was the new thing, and they were involved in it. It was much more than historical memory. They believed that what they had hoped for was not illusion, but was now reality. They were part of the new happening.

Before They Wrote It Down

Jesus himself had written nothing. There was a period when nothing was written down about Jesus. But as the early Christians began to worship Jesus Christ they not only remembered his sayings, but they also wrote them down for others. There is good reason to think that short manuals with 'sayings of Jesus' began circulating in the very early days of the church's history.

When the apostles and eyewitnesses began to die, or were put to death, it became important to preserve their knowledge and understanding of Jesus. So a new kind of writing, called Gospel, came into being. *Mark*, the earliest of those that now remain to us, was written about A.D. 65 — many years after the event. The remembering came first. Then came the writing as the different sources were gathered together.

Deliberate and Selective Remembering

The Gospel writers deliberately selected and arranged the traditions about Jesus and explicitly stated they had done so (*Luke* 1:1-3; *John* 20:3, 31). The question arises, What was the basis for the inclusion or exclusion of a particular story or statement? Basically it was the relevance of the material to the church's needs, one of which was, by John's own admission (*John* 20:31), the adequate fulfilment of the missionary task. As the young church faced its particular problems as a community in the Roman world, it would recall what Jesus had said or done on different occasions. These recollections would help the church follow his will in the new situation it had to meet. So, we can almost feel the New Testament writers thinking as they addressed the different congregations and provided guidance upon the authority of Jesus Christ for the different kinds of problems that arose.

The selective remembering in the Gospels fixes a limit for our knowledge of Jesus, and the survival or perishing of such collections fixed a further limit. What these historical documents present is all that we can know of Jesus. Had the authors not written down what they did or if all of what they recorded had perished, we would not now be in a position to remember Jesus ourselves unless a very reliable oral tradition had been maintained from that day to this. So we depend upon the Gospels. With them we reach boundaries of our historical evidence and the limit of our historical knowledge.

The Church and the Form of the Traditions

The church had influence in shaping the traditions about Jesus which came to be written as Gospels. They had influence in shaping the form of the traditions.

How do we find out what Jesus did, taught and what happened to him? In answering this question is there some basic principle to guide us?

The Gospels were written very much later than the time of Jesus. The Gospels themselves came from different areas and different decades of the first century. Meanwhile churches had been founded rather widely in the Roman world. They faced problems of different kinds. There was opposition and persecution by hostile enemies. There were inside disagreements in matters both of doctrine and conduct. There were varying interpretations and understandings of Christian faith and hope. In face of the threat and the rise of false teaching, it was important that an agreed right way of understanding became clear. Over a period of many decades, stories about Jesus were being handed down from the witnesses to the generations that followed. Eventually these were put into writing, into Greek, the lingua franca of the Roman world. The authors of the Gospels lived in particular places and situations at particular times. So from the situation and viewpoint of the different communities, what was remembered of Jesus' life, example teaching and death was appealed to as guidance and inspiration for the different Christian communities in their varying situations. So the teachings and remembrances became influential in guiding the early Christians in their belief and living. This was bound to be reflected in the documents which came out of the various situations. Each of the evangelists, in his writing, or compilation, reflected the varied situations of the different churches. So to get behind the early church to the historical Jesus, we must take account of interests and situations of the church as it can be discerned in these documents.

The Source Problem: 'This Generation'

The traditional reader could simply take a passage from the text of the Gospel and attribute the words of the text to Jesus. Now, we must take account of the source problem. The sources for understanding Jesus were written decades after he lived. They are documents featuring what was remembered in the Christian communities that emerged in the later first century, from around A.D. 65 to the end of the century. They represent the memories of the witnesses and the reports of their hearers.

The evangelists approached their materials from different points of view. So we must ask, 'How do we decide which saying had its source in the actual words of Jesus himself? Which of the sayings in some way reflect the church's understanding of his words, in the light of their particular situations?' We remember that the evangelist relied upon the memory of the witnesses. We remember also that Jesus spoke Aramaic and that the Gospels are written in Greek.

When you ask an historical question you must apply the methods of the historian to find an answer. When you ask an historical question that has to be answered by reference to written sources you have to apply the methods of the literary historian to find an answer. Both will refer to facts which can be established and will attempt to interpret the text in the light of these facts.

So the source problem can be expressed in the question, 'How do we decide which of the events and sayings found in these documents, now called Gospels, had their source in Jesus himself and which in the early church, including the evangelists, who relied upon the memory of the witnesses?' A generation and more was passing or had passed before the four Gospels had been compiled.

But what difference does it make? What is the relevance of all this to the question of eschatology? Simply this. As a result of this inquiry, we can affirm that Jesus was an eschatological preacher and also an eschatological figure.

Take an example or two bearing on our topic, eschatology. The passages in view refer to the coming of the Kingdom, the *parousia*.

'This generation shall not pass away till all these things shall be fulfilled.' *Matthew* 24:34. 'Truly I say to you, there are some standing here who will not taste death before they see the Son of man coming in his kingdom.' *Matthew* 16:27-28. Does it make a difference whether the sayings are the actual precise words of Jesus or words as remembered by the disciples and believers who had witnessed them?

Taking these words as actually spoken by Jesus, they clearly indicate that the time of the visible, glorious return of Christ is fixed within limits, not far ahead. They also indicate quite clearly that Jesus was an eschatological figure, announcing the coming of the end. Other passages confirm this, as well as terms used by Jesus, e.g. Son of Man.

The event will take place within the present generation of Jewish life, indeed within the life span of Jesus' hearers. The limit is clearly demarcated, the boundary definitely fixed. So failure of the event to take place will represent a major crisis for believers, by showing the prediction to have been false. So does the hope find its final expression in the words of the conclusion of the book of *Revelation*? 'He which testifieth these things saith, Surely I come quickly. Amen. Even so, come, Lord Jesus.' *Revelation* 22:20. Do those words represent the last expression of the hope for the *parousia* before the final disappearance of 'this generation'? Could they represent the final expression of one of those who was 'standing there'?

The event to come is clearly demarcated within a particular time limit, 'this generation', the lifetime of 'some standing here.'

The time of the visible, glorious return and setting up of the Kingdom is fixed within a limit, not far ahead, as it had often been by the apocalyptists. Since it is clearly bounded, if it does not take place within the bounds that failure to happen will constitute the great disappointment of the primitive apostolic church, and set a pattern for all future such hopes of the church through the centuries with similar expectation. There came a point in the experience of the first century church when its members had to come to terms with the non-occurrence of the *parousia*.

DISCUSSION QUESTIONS
Chapter 2

(1) In what ways are the Gospels the primary witnesses to the life and teachings of Jesus?

(2) How did the early church come to terms with the non-occurrence of the *parousia*?

3

NEW TESTAMENT ESCHATOLOGY

A Sampling

We shall now provide a sampling of New Testament understandings relevant to our discussion of eschatology. It is a sketch that focuses on three themes:

Jesus as an eschatological figure.

The eschatological understanding of the existence and faith of the church.

Apocalyptic as expressing the ultimate eschatological hope of the consummation at the end (both *finis* and *telos*).

The early church expected the *parousia*, but the *parousia* did not happen. But no crisis took place. How did the church come to terms with the delay of the *parousia*? How did the church relate to the *eschaton*?

The answer is that there was no single, uniform attempt to solve the problem. The situations of the various churches were different and as time passed they faced different problems. What became plain was that the church would continue to exist and would come to terms with the fact of its continuing existence. The fact is that the church did not retreat from the world, as did the Gnostics, but reckoned with life in the world.

So it faced different situations and problems. There was the delay of the *parousia*. There were enthusiastic believers in an immediate *parousia*. There were incipient heresies, not the least of a Gnostic kind, denying all connection of faith with history. Nero (A.D. 64-65) and Domitian (A.D. 95-96) were deliberately active in persecuting Christians, who came to be regarded as enemies of the Republic.

Paul in *I Thessalonians* expressed belief that the Advent is to be within the lifetime of some believers, 'we which are alive and remain'. But there is no need for believers to worry about dates and times. Even here 'eschatology is not primarily an apocalyptic conception, but an understanding of being in faith.[1]

The book of *Revelation* employs apocalyptic material to create the 'drama of the end'. Christ reigns in Heaven. Satan has been cast out. The end is near. The book of Hebrews envisages the people of God holding firm to faith in their time of wandering. 'Under the token of immediate expectation, the epistle prepares its readers in reality for the long period of striving and suffering'.[2] When persecution takes place the expectation of immediate release at the *parousia* gets intensified, as is evident from *I Peter*. 4:7.

In *Colossians* salvation is now, in the present. Against Gnostic tendencies, e.g. to speak of salvation as automatic, it insists that salvation took place historically, through the 'historical saving act of the cross'.[3] Christ sustains the creation. Nothing is outside the scope of Christ's redemptive work. The cross is central to redemption. In *Ephesians,* the time factor is similarly excluded. The mystery has now been revealed. Salvation is now.

For *Matthew* the church is the true Israel. Israel refused the revelation of God. The church maintains a continuity with Israel, but replaces the nation in terms of promise and fulfilment. The Son of Man sows the good seed. The church awaits the fulfilment. Judgement is at the end. It is not the prerogative of the church now to administer it. It faces its continuing and emerging problems of persecution and of heresy. Present and future are in dialectic relationship. The church has authority now 'to bind and to loose. . . .' *Matthew* 18:18. The church must deal with its problems now, but also await the future for 'heaven' to produce the final judgement. In

---

1   Hans Conzelmann, *An Outline of the Theology of the 'New Testament*. p. 308.
2   *Ibid.*, p. 312.
3   *Ibid.*, p. 315.

Eschatology

the meantime it does not separate itself from the world and become an apocalyptic sect. It lives in the world and does its best to regulate its affairs in matters of teaching and practice.[1]

In the *Gospel of John, parousia,* judgement and resurrection are not excluded, but integrated into his understanding of salvation as present. The believer has life. In the future he will continue to have what he already has. What is in prospect is the 'final return and presence of Jesus for faith'.[2]

In *Luke* the expectation of an imminent end is replaced by a picture of salvation history. Luke sees the answer to the problem of the non-appearance of the *parousia* by interpreting the intervening time as the period of the church. The time between resurrection and *parousia* will be long. But the kingdom exists beyond time and will surely come. The Jewish community held fast to the expectation that a prophet would appear at the end time, the time of restoration.[3] After the long space of time when there was none, the coming of a prophet will let them know that the end-time, the time of restoration, had come. So when John the Baptist appeared, it gave the assurance that that time had come. God was speaking now through the prophet again. The appearance of the prophet is itself a fulfilment of prophecy. This is indicated by Luke's quotation of the passage in *Isaiah,* 'all mankind shall see God's deliverance . . . .' *Luke* 3:2-6.

---

1 *Ibid.,* pp. 144-149.

2 *Ibid.,* p. 357.

3 During the time of the Maccabees, in the midst of all the destruction, including the desolation of the temple, the expectation was voiced that a prophet would appear. He would restore temple worship. Meanwhile the people appointed a leader until such time when a true prophet should appear (*I Maccabees* 4 :44 ff, 14:41). The psalmist in the same context expresses the same sentiment as he mourns, 'We have no prophet now.' *Psalm* 74:9. So when God speaks through his prophets again, the end time will have come.

Cosmic Significance

It is clear from several passages in the New Testament that the question was raised and conviction expressed that the Christ-event had cosmic significance. Jesus Christ is related to the beginning, the creation of all things.[1]

It is here a question not of providing a *Weltanschauung*, a theoretical account of the beginning of all things within the context of a scientific account of the universe, but of self-understanding.[2] I do not argue to the conclusion that God is Creator of the world. As I respond to the message of God's saving grace I come to the understanding that this is God's world, that the world is God's creation. Given also with this understanding is that the world is to reach its consummation as a creative act of God. My awareness is one of standing in a history which is the scene of God's revelation.[3] Jesus Christ the Son is creative not only in the midst of that history but also at its beginning and at its end. That I escape the 'realm of darkness' means that through Christ God has chosen to 'reconcile the whole universe to himself'. Such an understanding stood in opposition to the non-historical view of the Gnostics.

The Little Apocalypse

In the spring of 70 A. D. Titus and his legions arrived before the walls of Jerusalem. After a five month siege, and the final desperate stand in the Temple by the Jews, the city fell to the Romans who murdered, plundered and then destroyed it by fire. It was the culmination of a long period of misrule, revolt, sacrilege and often,

---

1   *I Corinthians* 8:6; *John* 1:1-3; *Ephesians* 1:9,10; *Colossians* 1:13-20.
2   'I cannot understand my existence as dependent on God unless I understand my being as created by God and destined for God.' The faith that God revealed himself in history 'relates the cosmos to history'. Emil Brunner, *The Christian Doctrine of the Church, Faith, and the Consummation*, pp. 427, 429.
3   To follow up the implications of this claim see my *History and Christian Faith*.

Eschatology

on the part of the Jews, fanatical resistance against the Romans, encouraged by early successes.

This event features in the writings of the evangelists, *Mark, Matthew* and *Luke*.

Stories and accounts about the life and teaching of Jesus had been circulating before this time. There were many of these. They have now come to be called *pericopai* (the plural of *pericope*). They circulated here and there throughout the world and as time passed they were put into some shape by being collected together and edited. In this way our Gospels came into being. There is much repetition between the synoptic Gospels, sometimes verbatim and sometimes with significant amendments and additions. Dates for the Gospels are: *Mark* A. D. 65-70, *Luke* A. D. 75-85, *Matthew* A. D. 85-90.[1]

Much of *Mark* is to be found in *Matthew* and *Luke*. Frequently the words are identical. Such identity suggests a literary relation. *Matthew* and *Luke* often duplicate material that is not in *Mark*. We find this illustrated in what has come to be called the Little Apocalypse. This term refers to *Mark* 13, *Matthew* 24-25 and *Luke* 21.

We now look at what *Mark* said in anticipation of the coming of the Kingdom, the end of all things, the *eschaton*. Now we meet with apocalyptic themes. The heavenly bodies will take extraordinary courses, followed by the coming of the Son of Man, and the gathering of the elect from all quarters of the globe (verses 24-27).[2] These are undated predictions. The time of the Advent is unknown. Only God the Father knows that (v.32). Parallels to *Mark* are found in *Matthew* and *Luke*. The admonition is then given that one must be ever alert in view of the possibility of a surprise *parousia*. The end is near, but 'near' is undefined.[3]

---

[1] It is not within the scope of this writing to treat this interesting topic at length. There is a wealth of literature on the subject, which can be approached on different levels.

[2] Destruction of Jerusalem: verses 1-14, 17-23, 28-31. End of the Age: verses 15-16, 24-27, 32-37.

[3] Parallels to *Mark* are found in *Matthew* and *Luke*.

What then is the relation between the destruction of the Temple and the End of the Age? Does the End of the Age follow immediately after the destruction of Jerusalem and the Temple? Or, are the two events to be separated eschatologically and temporarily? Was *Mark* somewhat indifferent, so that we cannot say what his understanding of their relation was? Or, have the two events been tied together more closely than they should have been?[1]

What is most probable is that *Mark* took no stand on the temporal relation between the events of the destruction of Jerusalem and the End and that he was urging his readers to constant and diligent discipleship. The Kingdom will come. In the meantime God is active. What is now hidden will be revealed. In the meantime there is to be patience and assurance that the future is in the hands of God. It is noticeable that he does not encourage an immediate expectation of the *parousia* to follow the events of A.D. 70.

The *Gospel of Matthew* demonstrates a particular interest in Judaism. It quotes frequently from the Old Testament. It sees Jesus prefigured therein, and Christianity as the fulfilment of Judaism. He shows a particular interest in eschatology. In his 'little apocalypse' of chapter 24, the references in *Mark* are given greater emphasis. Everything is related to the coming of the Son of Man. The term *parousia* occurs in the Gospels only in *Matthew*.

Luke has expanded Mark's account adding 'signs' of the coming (verses 9-11, 25-26). Luke wrote after the destruction of Jerusalem and gives a precise account of what happened to the inhabitants (verses 21-24). So we are to take the signs as referring not to the fall of the city, but as anticipating the coming of the Son of Man (verses 9-11, 25-27). But there is no clear-cut distinction between predictions regarding the Temple and Jerusalem and apocalyptic signs and the coming of the Son of Man.

Luke was a Gentile. His interest is to show how the Christian church was progressing in the Roman world. His outlook is described as 'salvation-historical.' There will be a long period before the end of the world. That is the time of the church, which is active

---

1 Geddert, T. J. *Mark 13,* 1989, pp. 253-45.

in the interim between the resurrection and the *parousia*. The time of the end we do not know. 'Luke has understood that the expectation of an imminent end cannot be continued. . . . [N]ot only does the expectation of an imminent end simply disappear, but it is replaced by a picture of salvation history.[1]

---

1 *An Outline of the Theology of the New Testament*, pp. 149-150.
  Luke portrays the story of salvation between two limits, the Creation and the Parousia. Between these limits there are three successive periods, the period of Israel, that of the Law and the Prophets; the period of Jesus; the last period of the church and of the Spirit. He does not say that this period will be short. There is no speculation that we are getting nearer to the end. We are warned not to calculate. Hans Conzlemann, *The Theology of St. Luke*. p. 150. For commentary on *Luke* 21, cf. pp. 95-132, contained within the section 'Luke's eschatology'. pp. 95-136.

DISCUSSION QUESTIONS
Chapter 3

(1) Define carefully the terms eschatology, apocalyptic.

(2) Does eschatology have to do only with the future?

(3) 'Eschatology is not primarily an apocalyptic conception, but an understanding of being in faith.' Explore the meaning of this statement.

(4) Describe and explain the different approaches to the New Testament writers to the subject of the expectation of the Advent.

(5) What does it mean to speak of 'salvation history' in *Luke*?

4

Prophecy And Apocalyptic

Argument from Prophecy

In conservative evangelical circles the argument from prophecy is still very much alive, as we shall see. But one theologian, expressing the conviction of many, wrote that it has become established in twentieth century theology, that 'this kind of argument from prophecy can no longer be used in the service of the Lord of truth'.[1]

The idea is that centuries before the events took place the prophet foresaw what was to be and wrote it down for the edification of the reader. In particular he saw the advent of Jesus and predicted events of his life and death. So the Christian, as indeed the Jew before him, might see that God was operative in human history. For the Christian this also involved that God was in Christ ordaining the salvation of the human. A widely held idea was that the Bible was a divinely given written record of revelation. For many this meant that God had dictated the words of revelation. However a verbal doctrine of the inspiration of the Bible was not essential to conviction of its inerrancy. But however the words got to the papyrus and finally to the India paper, they were to be taken literally.

---

1 Alan Richardson, *Christian Apologetics*. London: S. C. M. Press, 1947. pp. 178-180. 'So long as it was possible to think of the Bible as a divinely dictated written record of revelation, it was possible to understand prophecy as a matter of the detailed fulfilment of predictions contained in particular verses or passages of the Old Testament: but with the abandonment of such a theory of biblical inspiration a different view of the nature of the fulfilment of prophecy is required.'

The Hebrew word for 'prophet' means 'spokesman', whatever he utters, whether it had reference to the present, to the past, or to the future. He was the voice of God in the Hebrew community, and was often the most important person in the land, even with more influence than the king. Indeed frequently he set his message in opposition to that of the king and his associates.

There are various strands to the traditional argument.

(1) The first is that the spokesman, the writer, spoke of events in advance of his time, often long in advance of his time.

(2) He wrote down his predictions, sometimes centuries, even millennia, before they would take place, often giving surprising detail.

(3) The events predicted in due course actually took place, not once only but regularly. The reliability of the predictions could therefore be relied upon. If the prophet predicted an event, that event could be reckoned with.

(4) These events were happenings within human history and so could be attested by witnesses and recorded by the historian. Over and over again, then, the word of prophecy showed itself to be 'sure' and reliable.

(5) Particular and specific prophecies were 'fulfilled' in the life of Jesus of Nazareth. This was recognised by New Testament writers who testify to a connection between the Old Testament oracle and the life and meaning of Jesus. From their experience of Jesus they then discerned that the prophet's words were appropriate to describe their understanding of Jesus. That does not mean, for example, that the prophets had divine and so miraculous foreknowledge of the events, say as Matthew's Gospel portrays them. What was latent in the Old Testament becomes patent in the New. The New Testament writer

sees a meaning that the Old Testament writer suggests to him. For example *Isaiah* 7:14 states, 'A woman shall conceive and bear a son'. The original words had reference to an imminent threat of desolation to Judah. The prophet warns, Before the child born to the woman comes to maturity, the land will be desolate. *Matthew* now gives a quite new application to the words, 'A woman will conceive and bear a son' gets now applied to the birth of Jesus and to the mother Mary, who as a virgin, will bear a son. The original words are taken as prophetic of this later event, even if intended for a former one, They are given a new meaning. For *Matthew* and for Christians this was the significant one. So one applies the idea of fulfilment of prophecy to the event now seen as the meaning of the oracle.

(6) The 'argument from prophecy' as it was called rests upon a particular view of scriptural inspiration and in turn the appeal to fulfilment demonstrates the divine nature of the Bible. For such predictive capacity is far beyond the capacity of the merely human. So appeal to the fulfilment of prophecy reinforces the status of biblical inspiration and authority from which it is derived. One can literally compare the prophecies of the Old Testament with their fulfilment in the New.

(7) But there remain the many proposed prophecies that have not been as yet fulfilled. All the predictions may be classified into two kinds, those that refer to events within the world, within human history, and those that have reference to events to take place in the transcendent world. This leads to the next stage of the confirming argument.

Since we have been convinced that 'there is a more sure word of prophecy' by witnessing the fulfilment of predictions within the world of our experience, we may rest assured that we can rely on those other predictions that have reference to events and activities in the transcendent world. Events in our human history can act as signs of the proximity of the 'last things'. These 'signs of the times' give assurance to the believer who hopes for the soon return of Jesus Christ, the imminent Second Advent.

On the Anselmian understanding[1] of incarnation and salvation, transactions have taken place between Father and Son in the heavens. Such arrangements mean that God the Father is able to pardon sinners on account of the activity of the Son. But this needs post-resurrection negotiating to effect the desired result for man the sinful creature. This is achieved through the activity of the Son, former sacrifice, now high priest in the heavenly sanctuary. Now we enter the world of eschatology. For the eschatological events are transcendent. They have no source in human activity. They happen, are initiated and mostly take place in a transcendent realm.

(8) Apocalyptic is taken as a kind of prophecy, and the apocalyptic writings (at least those within the biblical canon) are treated in much the same way as the 'prophecies'. They point to real events, the sequence and

---

1 Anselm, *Cur Deus Homo*. This writing presents what has come to be called the satisfaction theory of the Atonement. God's justice, violated by man's sin, must be satisfied. The conditions for that satisfaction are that, since sin and death entered the world through a man, Adam, so redemption should take place through a man, Jesus. But only one who is God could achieve that satisfaction. So the agent of salvation must be the God-man. This requires the incarnation. As man, Jesus suffered and was obedient: 'the Father willed that the human race should not be restored, unless man should do some act as great as was that death' (Chapter 9). It is a question of restoring honour to God, an honour violated by man's sin. The debt to God that sinful man has incurred robbed God of his due honour. But God is merciful and in his mercy, when offered the sacrifice of the Son, he can forgive the whole debt. God's justice is thus satisfied. In this way, Anselm claims, the satisfaction of God's justice is shown to be rational.

details of which can be elaborated from the apocalyptic writing. Such events now observed to have taken place indicate the imminence of the final events.

The Prophet's Problem

Before an event happens we may or may not know that it is going to happen. Our degree of certainty will depend on the nature of the event and the evidence we have for the probability of its taking place. It will also depend upon the attitude of the subject, since certainty is a psychological phenomenon. The simple-minded may well be certain, the hard empiricist not.

Our attitude will most certainly be determined by our past experience. The range of our experience will measure how extensive is the range of our testimony and thus of our expectations, and the reliability of our predictions.

After an event has happened we may or may not be able to know that it has happened. What is clear is that we can only know that an event has happened when it has happened. But an event may have happened and we are not able to know that it has happened, or what it was that happened. We may not know that some event took place, nor be able to specify the features of the event. Historians must plead ignorance for events beyond the grasp of interpreted evidence. The event took place, but is now inaccessible. Sometimes we cannot say what happened. Sometimes we cannot say that something happened. That is the problem of the historian and the detective.

But some events are beyond the range of our experience. We make predictions about this kind of event very precariously. That is the problem of the prophet and the prophetically inclined. So what does that mean for the prophet and for those communities founded on the claim to be able to predict the future? Sometimes the predictions refer to ordinary terrestrial events. Sometimes they refer to trans-terrestrial events, the super-terrestrial. The events predicted may also be supernatural events taking place within the world.

Prophecy and prediction are a part of our lives. Ask the economist, the sports commentator, the gambler, the weather forecaster, the investor, the pollster. You may not want to ask the politicians. But that won't make any difference. They will go on making forecasts. In their own way, of course!

But we should know how to evaluate the predictions we hear and those we make, as does the scientist, since prediction is part and parcel of his game. A basic part of the strategy of the physical scientist is to set up conditions, make predictions and then devise the means by which such predictions may be tested and the results examined for further research. Needless to say, such work is done on the assumption that empirical testing is available for such predictions. An hypothesis remains an hypothesis until the evidence either falsifies it or fails to verify it.

The prophet is in a peculiar position. For to know that the prediction is true would be to have experienced the event predicted. To believe that the prediction is probable would entail that one have had experience in a class with that of the predicted event. All other considerations would render at best some degree of probability that the event will take place. So to predict an event of a certain kind, say an earthquake, the prophet is able to make reference to preceding similar events and to amass a whole range of data bearing on the claim. But whether the resultant claim is true will depend upon the actual experiencing of the event that has been predicted or on the reliability of the testimony to the event. Reliable evidence will be available at some point. The event will have to occur or to have occurred to verify the prediction.

In the religious context many predictions are not like that. There is in many cases no way of appealing to the occurrence of similar events that indicate that it will take place, for in the nature of the case, the event predicted is totally unique. So there can be no argument such as the following:

Some events are similar to the predicted event.

Events similar to the predicted event have occurred.

Other phenomena were present when these events occurred

(such phenomena have been researched.)

Since similar phenomena are now present, we can safely make a predictive hypothesis.

Therefore the event predicted is probable.

We could only tell whether the event predicted took place 'soon' after the prediction, when we examined how much preceding time there was before its occurrence. We can obviously only do that if and when the event has actually taken place. So even if we allow that 'soon' is to be taken to mean 'one hundred years from now', i.e. A. D. 2112, we shall only be able to verify or to falsify the claim after that time has elapsed, and we arrive at the date predicted. If 'soon' means 'at some time in the indefinite future', there is no way of verifying or falsifying the sentence. That must be obvious, since no claim is being made.

Moreover if the predicted event is totally unique there is no way of appealing to preceding events, so as to provide some empirical evidence for its probability. No such coordination is possible. This observation would be true for a totally unique physical event within the cosmos. But we are here also dealing with supernatural events whose origin lies totally outside the realm of nature, in reality 'acts of God'!

So what if one claims that the great consummation involving the end of the present order will take place 'soon'? The Bible ends with the words 'Behold I come quickly.' Those words point to a culmination, bringing to its fulfilment what the book of *Revelation* has in symbolic terms predicted: the triumph of good over evil. It is a word of consolation to those whose suffering it has portrayed, but whose ultimate triumph has been assured. Much of the symbolism of the book portrays the intensity of the experience of the community of believers in the time before that ultimate triumph. But the relation between what precedes the final triumph and the *parousia* is not one of normal, regular and therefore predictable effect following cause. It is the decisive and majestic 'act of God' that brings about the final denouement of human history. None of the preceding events give the answer to our question. The end is utterly and finally an 'act of God'. 'Behold I come quickly' (*nai erchomai tachu*). The Bible practically ends with the word 'soon' (*tachu*).

There is a traditional way of prophetic assurance, i.e. of guaranteeing that what is predicted is true, that the events predicted will come to pass. Since no empirical test is available or even possible in the present, that is to say before the predicted event will occur, the appeal is made to the certainty of revelation. The line of reasoning is this:

Let God be true.

God's truth is here revealed in an authoritative Scripture.

The revelation is in this prophecy.

Therefore this prophecy is true.

Therefore my certainty that it will be fulfilled is well founded.

Therefore the event will happen.

There is no need to appeal to evidence. You can make the prediction with full assurance, even if the predicted event may seem unlikely. But evidence is not necessary for one who has the conviction that the above argument provides.

Two concluding observations are appropriate.

Sometimes the prediction is of such a kind that we have to wait and see whether the event predicted does in fact happen. The prediction will be shown to be true if it does and false if it does not.

Some of the predicted events are beyond the range of empirical evidence since they are predicted to happen in the supernatural or transcendent sphere, a sphere to which as humans we do not have access. We have therefore no way of knowing whether the predicted event has taken place.

A warning is appropriate. There is an alternative way of thinking about fulfilment than looking for detailed fulfilment of predictions drawn from particular passages of Scripture, as was done to find specific fulfilments of the Old Testament in the life and fate of Jesus. With the demise of the inspiration theory a more appropriate understanding of fulfilment took place.[1]

---

1 See footnote 1 page 30.

Eschatology

Apocalyptic

Apocalypses[1] foretell the ultimate victory of the kingdom of God. The world is evil and violent. The context is of suffering, persecution, and death for the believer. Evil is ascendant and there seems to be little hope. Revolt is suppressed mercilessly. The future appears not bleak, but hopeless. But evil will not always prosper. A dominating common feature is that the victory of good over evil is secure. The enemies of righteousness will be vanquished after the continuing manifestation of the powers of evil. Apocalyptic is dualistic. It presents a great continuing contest between the good and evil powers with the assured victory of the good.

The New Age is about to dawn. God is about to intervene, The kingdom of God is imminent and shall be universal. The end is predicted as very near indeed. It is an anticipation of victory not defeat. God will triumph and live with his people thereafter. So God's people can take courage and have certain hope. The ultimate triumph of good over the evil, which evil is, at the time of writing, only too evident, is assured. Jewish apocalyptic literature was popular in times of persecution. It flourished during the time of Antiochus Epiphanes when the Maccabean revolt (166-160 B.C.) took place. One of these writings attained a place in the Hebrew canon, namely the book of *Daniel*. Features common to Jewish apocalyptic are also evident in the Christian Apocalypse, very clearly in the canonical book of *Revelation*.

The apocalyptic writings have certain common features. The writings make the basic claim that they reveal hidden secrets that God revealed to particular persons, from Adam to Ezra. So the names of these individuals are linked to the particular writings. These secrets relate in particular to the last things. They reveal the fulfilment of God's purpose from creation to the end time. But they are especially relevant to the time of the readers. At that time, the tension heightens, for the end is predicted as very near indeed.

---

[1] The term 'apocalypse' derives from the Greek word *apokalupsis*, meaning 'revelation', unveiling, removal of a concealing veil. Cf. *II Corinthians* 3:13-16.

The writings use the language of symbols: animal figures and features, dragon, bull, ram, lion, eagle, bear, great horn, ribs. The canonical book of *Daniel* depicts the four great empires, Babylon, Media, Persia and Greece as mighty beasts, drawing its pictures by elaborating natural species: lion with eagles' wings; bear with three ribs in its mouth, leopard with four wings, a fourth great beast with ten horns and great iron teeth (*Daniel* 7:4-7).

Stars represent fallen angels. The fall of the angels led by Azazel, the prince of the fallen angels, is represented by a star followed by many other stars falling from heaven (*I Enoch* 86). Conflict in the transcendent sphere between supernatural beings leads to victory and defeat, but not to a final resolution of the conflict. That resolution is what the Apocalyptists predict. This narrative of a host of supernatural beings in defeated conflict with the Creator appears in the canonical book of *Revelation*. There is war in heaven. Michael and his angels fight against the dragon, 'that old serpent', called the Devil and Satan, who is cast out of heaven with his angels (12:7-9).

Another feature of apocalyptic is its use of number symbolism: the number seven in particular. Then there is the reference to periods of time: e.g. in *Daniel*, 2300 days (8:14), seventy years, seventy weeks, seven weeks and threescore and two weeks (9:24, 25).

The era of the Apocalyptists was from 200 BC to AD 100. They were thus the successors to the prophets and repeated some of their themes: they condemned the godless. They predicted punishment. They uttered comforting words to those who were suffering at the hands of oppressors. Their main theses were (1) that the world was hopelessly corrupt, (2) with no remedy but destined for complete destruction, (3) so that a new age could begin, the age of Messiah. (4) God has pre-determined what would take place in the world. (5) The Apocalyptists were appointed by God to reveal to their fellows the secrets that he had revealed to them. (6) They express different views about death, judgement, resurrection, punishment, eternal bliss, eternal punishment. (7) In the later Jewish writings, under the influence of Persian thought, resurrection is connected with world conflagration and judgement.

Eschatology 37

The themes of Christian apocalypses[1] are thus not original. They are an inheritance from Israel. The mode of depicting the conquest of evil as the vanquishing of supernatural evil beings as well as the wickedness of human beings was a recurring theme of the Jewish apocalyptists. But there was one crucial difference. For the Christian the future which the Jewish apocalyptists anticipated has come to pass in the person of Jesus. He is the Son of Man. He is the Messiah. He is the 'one who cometh'. But there is more. The future fulfilment will come when, at the end of all things, the Kingdom will be established and God, the Creator, 'will be all in all.'

Apocalyptic writings are, by and large, pseudonymous.[2] Pseudonymity (as we have seen) means associating a name which is not that of the writer, redactor or editor with the writing he produces. Pseudonymity was a literary device employed by the Jewish apocalyptists. The author associated his writing with the name of a figure well accepted in the community. The purpose of presenting the material as that of the earlier writer, recognised and revered by the readers, was to ensure it had acceptance and authority. The later writer or editor interpreted the earlier writer as if an extension of his personality. This harmonised well with the Hebrew notion of corporate personality.

The prophetic canon was fixed by 200 B.C. Inspiration was thought to have ceased after Ezra, who came to Jerusalem in 397 B.C. So only writings written before that date or believed to have been so written could be accepted as inspired and authoritative. So the Apocalyptists claimed that the secret that had been revealed to a figure before that date had been held back, but that now its time had arrived. The secret was now to be revealed. So, for example, it was now time for the message attributed to Daniel to be made known. The personality and message of the predecessor could be transmitted through the later apocalyptic writer to the reader. So

---

1   In the New Testament: the Apocalypse of John, i.e. the book of *Revelation* and the 'Little Apocalypse', *Mark* 13.
2   D. S. Russell, *Between the Testaments*. London: S. C. M. Press, 1963. An excellent introduction to the Jewish inter-testamental literature. Cf. p.114 .

the 'mind and message' of *Daniel* could be interpreted to the reader through the later intermediary and accepted as on a par with the canonical writings.

There is an issue here, since it is obvious that the writing cannot be prophetic, i.e. a prediction of future events, if it is written after the events have happened. That is the reason the traditionalist refuses to accept the literary point concerning authorship which gives the writings a date later than the events it describes. Take the book to have been written in the sixth century B.C. and the events that it depicts from then to the second century are predictions. So the writing is prophetic, in the sense of anticipating the future events. But if the writing dates from the second century, then the events are in the past, and the book is not prophetic. In that case the argument from prophecy to the authority of the writer and the book is neutralised. If the writing is not prophetic then there is no argument from the certainty of the fulfilment of predictions to the inspiration and unique authority of the writing.

But nevertheless the teaching of the Apocalyptists about the end time, the coming of the Kingdom, judgement and the destruction of the evil retains its significance. For beyond the terrestrial events involving earthly authorities, the Apocalyptists foretell the triumph of God over evil. That has not yet taken place. That is always in the future. What the Apocalyptists urge is that it is not long into their future. The end, the victory is near. Anticipate the great cosmic victory of good, the triumph of God over evil. Take heart and be of good courage! But they do not specify how long the time of waiting will be.

Such themes were widespread and popular for centuries before they were Christianised. They were current as Jesus, the Jew, lived and taught and died. He was acquainted with their ideas. Apocalyptic was a very potent force in Jewish religious thought, with its emphasis on the theme that the present time is the time of the end and that God is about to create a new order. Apocalyptic also provided the first century church with the means for interpreting the significance of Jesus. First century Judaism expected a speedy consummation. Jesus shared this. God will intervene in human affairs and create an imminent end, a new heaven and a new earth. For the Apocalyptists the last times were now, the present times. Much of the language of the early Christians and of Jesus himself is apocalyptic language.

Apocalyptic literature expressed the hope of a future resurrection. With that hope went also the idea of final judgement. For the righteous this meant transformation from present existence to an existence like the angelic beings. This hope was developed by the first century A.D. writings. It finds expression in Paul, who associated it with the resurrection of Jesus. Belief in a final resurrection is for Paul the presupposition for the resurrection of Jesus. 'For if the dead rise not, then is Christ not risen' (*I Corinthians* 15:16).

Interpreting the Apocalypse

Preterist, Futurist

The New Testament contains an Apocalypse, the book of *Revelation*. The question is, 'What shall we do with it? How shall we interpret it?' There is one important preliminary question we have to answer, 'Shall we in the twenty-first century take it as having its primary application to the past, the first temporal context in which it was composed?' Or shall we take it not as having an immediate application but one for the future, not least the very last of the generations before the great deliverance, at the actual end of all things? Words have been given to designate these different methods of interpretation. The preterist (referring to the past) understanding stands in contrast to the futurist.

The preterist interpretation asks what application the writings have to the community living at the time of the writing. The futurist interpretation takes the writing as predicting events from the time of writing to the *eschaton* and beyond. The futurist creates a complex system by interpreting the multiple and elaborate symbols of the book as having reference to real persecuting powers from ancient though medieval times to the present. What results provides for an understanding of significant events for the church in the course of history from the time of writing to the present. So observations can be made about the significance of the present state of affairs in the world. Since these are drawn from Scripture, as the symbols are interpreted, they have a special status, namely that of revealed truth. Such predicted recent events may then be taken as signs of the end. This in turn leads to the announcement that the consummation, the last judgement and the renewal of all things is at hand. We have seen that this is a feature of apocalyptic.

For many, such a sequence is convincing and comforting, giving assurance of consummation and fulfilment on a universal, cosmic scale. Moreover, the beleaguered Christian community rests convinced that after intense persecution by the evil powers, secular and apostate, it shall ultimately triumph.

Between the writing of the book, — say 100 A.D. — and the present time, Christian interpreters have found fulfilments relating to the rise of persecuting powers and the people of God, the true church. Both secular and religious powers plot and execute harm against God's people. The symbols invite application to the threat that is contemporary to a particular time. The symbols are taken to be previewing the evil and encouraging the good in many different but similar contexts, as one age gives place to another.

It is no secret that Protestants have found in the Apocalypse descriptive predictions of the Papacy as the persecuting power that engaged in violent opposition to dissenters. That application might be avoided if the preterist interpretation of the book were assumed. The writing was relevant for the church contemporary with the writing, in the context of the persecution by the Roman emperors. The symbols could not then be applied to the Middle Ages and the Inquisition. Reference to the Papacy was thus avoided.

DISCUSSION QUESTIONS
Chapter 4

(1) Outline the traditional 'argument from prophecy'.

(2) What differences are there between prophecy and apocalyptic, between prophet and apocalyptist?

(3) What did the chapter say was 'the prophet's problem'? Discuss.

(4) Explain the following terms: pseudonymous, pre-determination, fulfilment, prophetic canon, preterist, futurist.

(5) How do you think that the book of *Revelation* has been relevant in each age of the Christian church?

5

ESCHATOLOGY AND THE QUEST

The Jesus of History and Christian Faith

You do not have to read very much about eschatology before you come across the distinction between the Jesus of history and the Christ of Faith. So there is a basic question to be answered. For there seems to be a separation between what can be said about the historical figure of Jesus that the historian discovers from the sources, i.e. the Gospels, and the Jesus proclaimed by the apostles and believed on in the early church as we gather this from the writings of the New Testament.

What, if any, is the connection between the Jesus whom the historian finds, using the tools which he employs in assessing historical documents and in presenting historical events and figures of the past, and the Christ as proclaimed in the apostolic church and in all later Christian preaching, the Christ of the preacher and the pew?

This proclamation is now called *kerygma*. This term has two meanings: (1) the content of the proclamation; (2) the act of proclamation. In and as a result of the act of proclaiming the message about Jesus, the revelation of God took place and Christian faith was the result. So we must distinguish between the teaching of Jesus, the actual words he spoke, and the message that the church spoke and heard about Jesus.

What has all this to do with eschatology? Simply this, that the message about Jesus included an eschatological element at its core.

The crucified, resurrected Jesus will come again and the end will be soon. As we examine the Gospels asking, 'What do we know about the historical Jesus?' we are confronted with a preacher of eschatological themes: Son of Man, Kingdom of God, and expectation of the end: 'This generation shall not pass till all these things shall be fulfilled.'

Take for example the term 'Son of Man'. The first thing to be said of the Son of Man is that he is a eschatological figure.[1] As such he is associated with the eschatological transformation. This eschatological activity is his true task. His real work belongs to the last times. That comment has reference to Jewish apocalyptic, the following to the book of *Revelation:* 'The Revelation of St. John is in accord with the late Jewish apocalypses on the question of the Son of Man, particularly striking in the great picture of the last judgement. . . . the part played by Christ corresponds exactly to the Son of Man in apocalyptic.'[2]

'What is expressed by all these titles, Son, only son, Son of God, Son of Man, Messiah, is that Jesus is the eschatological salvation-bringer, that his coming is the eschatological event.' With Jesus' coming, judgement takes place. This is thematic in the *Gospel of John*. Men are judged as they respond to the word of Jesus.

So the church, in responding to Jesus and in due course proclaiming the word about him, becomes the eschatological community. As such it awaits the final events when the Son of Man will destroy the wicked and save the righteous.

How then can the question arise, 'Does the Jesus of History have relevance for Christian faith?' What happened in theological discussion to raise this question to a central position? For traditional Christianity the question, 'What connection has the kerygmatic Christ to the historical Jesus?' would be unintelligible.[3] To the lay-

---

1 Sigmund Mowinckel, *He that Cometh*. Translated by G. W. Anderson. Oxford: Basil Blackwell, 1959, pp. 358-389.
2 Rudolf Bultmann, *New Testament Theology Vol. 2*, pp. 37-38.
3 You simply make a compendium of the four Gospels to achieve a narrative of the life of Jesus, adding details not given in the Gospels to fill out the story.

man today it is more than puzzling, even absurd. So you have to be ready to review, even if simply, the paths that Christian and other scholars have travelled in the last couple of centuries. The quest is to find Jesus as an historical figure. This involves a reassessment of the meaning of the 'end', the *eschaton*. In the process of this reassessment the two themes will be closely correlated: the historical Jesus and the *eschaton*.

Albert Schweitzer

Jesus proclaims that with him the Kingdom of God is breaking into the world. In doing so, he is himself the eschatological event. To realise this is to begin to understand the idea of eschatology.

Earlier there was a serious attempt to discover a different Jesus, who came to be called the 'Jesus of history'. This was called the Jesus of history movement, the 'Quest of the Historical Jesus'. The incentive behind this movement was to discover the real Jesus, a figure who could be established by historical research. This would then provide a ground for faith, and in doing so free the church from the tyranny of dogma. The 'historical Jesus' would provide an alternative to the Jesus Christ of the tradition, which defined him as one person with a divine and human nature.

This incentive provided impetus to the Quest. To discover the historical Jesus would be to anchor faith in a secure foundation. It gave rise to the important question, What is the relation between historical research and its results and Christian faith? That was an additional question to the discussion about the legitimacy of the applying historical criticism to the Scriptures. If you find the historical Jesus, what relation if any can he have to the emergence and continuance of Christian faith? Martin Kähler addressed the problem in no uncertain terms and tones.

The so-called 'Quest of the Historical Jesus' occupied some of the best exploratory minds of the nineteenth century.

It was not only Christian believers who were exercised by this question. One of the first to raise the issues quite clearly and with

---

An example of this is E. G. White *The Desire of Ages*.

great pains was not a believer. Reimarus, earlier (1774-78), had seen some of the basic issues clearly, and expressed them with great clarity.[1] He had anticipated some of the issues which Christian scholars and theologians were later to pursue at great length.

Albert Schweitzer documented the story of the 'Quest' in his monumental writing, named in its English Version, 'The Quest of the Historical Jesus'. He saw the prolonged effort as a great achievement, but a monumental failure. Later Christian leaders were to agree. The 'real' Jesus (as he was sometimes called) eluded all attempts to discover and portray him. However, what was made quite clear was that he was an eschatological figure. As such he challenged values of the contemporary post-Reformation theologians, who found in Jesus a world-accepting ethic and who accommodated his teaching to it. Protestantism was then out of sympathy with the world-negating spirit of Jesus. The conclusion was clear. Jesus is ruler rather than teacher, and nineteenth century religion had no way of expressing a contemporary understanding of him. It was becoming clear that it was Jesus' eschatological presence and pronouncements that constituted his revolutionary impact among his contemporaries.

Traditional and later conservative Christian belief gave a negative answer to the question about this historical questioning. The Bible was authoritative and was not to be submitted to the investigations of the historians. 'Is the Bible to be subjected to the same canons of historical study' as are applied to other documents? Are 'the same methodological canons' as were applied to other religious traditions and scriptures to be applied to the Christian scriptures? The critic said 'yes'. The traditionalist insisted that the Bible was a holy and infallible book. So, regarded as such it was not to be subjected to the investigative methods of the historian. Whatever was required to be true for belief was to be shielded from critical assessment. The basic point in question was that faith had a decisive place in assessing the truth of biblical statements. What was

---

1   Reimarus, *Fragments. Edited by Charles H. Talbert,* Translated by Ralph S Fraser. London: S. C. M. Press, 1971.

Eschatology 47

demanded by belief was to be put beyond examination. The claim that challenged this was the basic principle of the historian: 'faith has no function in the justification of historical arguments respecting fact.'[1] So the critical study of the historical data raised serious questions about the presuppositions of the conservative believer. A basic assumption of the historical approach to Scripture was that there could be no special method peculiar to the believer as he worked with the canonical documents of the Christian community. If the traditionalists claimed immunity from such investigation, they were seriously in error.

Martin Kähler

Martin Kähler finds that the uniqueness of Scripture remains unaffected by the critical work of scholars. The Bible is witness to God's revelation. Hence there is a relationship between faith and the Bible, such as there is not between faith and other documents. There is risk, of course, in such questioning since the church is raising the question about its own foundation.

Martin Kähler quite deliberately presented his view of the Bible as an alternative to two particular teachings. The first of these was that the origin of the writings and hence their inerrancy is guaranteed by verbal inspiration. However the second alternative view that Kähler also finds unsatisfactory, claims that the historical study in particular of the Gospels can provide a basis for faith in God by demonstrating a '. . . historical connection between the biblical writings and those persons and events credited with the mediation of divine revelation. . . .'[2] This was unsatisfactory because it put the authority of the Bible at the mercy of historical research, 'documentary research'. The function of the Gospels is to 'awaken faith in Jesus through a clear proclamation of his saving activi-

---

1 The issue has been presented over and over again. For an interesting analysis see Van A. Harvey, *The Historian and the Believer*, Chapter IV, pp. 102-126. The quotation is from p. 112.
2 *The So-called Historical Jesus and the Historic Biblical Christ*, p. 107.

ty'.¹ Historical research was unable to provide a definitive account of Jesus. If you cannot have a definitive historical reconstruction you cannot rest your faith upon the results of any such attempt to reconstruct. Kähler's particular concern was with the historical Jesus. The purpose of the Gospels is not to provide a source for historical research, but to provide for faith in Jesus Christ. Scripture provides the ground for Christian proclamation, and it is through such proclamation that God reveals himself and that faith comes to be. 'That', says Kähler, 'should constitute sufficient theological justification for assigning a special authority to Scripture.'² It also rescues Christ from the scholars and makes him available to all Christians.³

Higher Criticism⁴

The documents of the Judaeo-Christian tradition, including the apocalyptic writings (not all of which became canonical Scripture), were the subject of serious investigation. The question of the authorship of the writings was addressed as the principles of historical investigation were being applied. This was regarded as perverse by conservative Christians with regard to their canonical books. Critical attitudes to authorship and to the source of materials contained in the books were in many cases dismissed as pernicious and perverse. The 'higher critics' were summarily rejected in certain quarters, lampooned and caricatured. They were not immune from a bizarre kind of mockery.

---

1   *Ibid., p. 127.*
2   *Ibid., p. 129.*
3   *Ibid., p. 102.*
4   The term 'higher' in contrast to 'lower' when used of literary criticism has to do with the position taken in reference to the text. Lower criticism deals with the text lower down the chain of production, so with the actual words and chapters as they are to be found in any particular version. Higher criticism deals with questions about the coming into being of the text and addresses itself to such questions as, When was the text produced? What are the sources of the text? How are the sources of the text related to the resulting text?

The question of date as well as authorship was analysed. This, as we have seen, is of particular interest in regard to apocalyptic books interpreted as predicting events far beyond the time of writing.

To preserve the authenticity of the predictions of world domination that the writings bearing the name of Daniel were asserted to contain, they had to be dated long before the second century B.C. A later date would mean that they were reports rather than predictions. That would mean a quite different function for them. This result entails that grand schemes of world history read from the pages of *Daniel* were quite unacceptable. Predictions of world history on the basis of the writing were no longer possible.

We will finally note just two points.

(1) The literary historian does not presuppose that the writing must be predictive. That he finds to be a gratuitous assumption. He produces evidence by rejecting that hypothesis. Rather he looks to other alternatives, for example, that many apocalyptic writings he examines are associated with accepted figures from past history. The prevalence of such pseudepigraphy (false claims to authorship) was a common phenomenon, in particular with apocalyptic writings.

(2) To predict in detail, centuries in advance, is highly improbable. A human being is not capable of such detailed knowledge.

DISCUSSION QUESTIONS
Chapter 5

(1) What do the following terms mean: proclamation, *kerygma*, the Jesus of history, the Christ of faith?

(2) Why was the 'Quest of the Historical Jesus' important? What is its significance for the topic of eschatology?

(3) What are they and what are the methods and aims of: a. Higher criticism b. Lower criticism?

6

ESCHATOLOGY
FUTURE AND PRESENT

Types of Eschatology

Christian theology is essentially eschatology. 'From the beginning, eschatology is not primarily an apocalyptic conception, but an understanding of being in faith.' The question then is, Which eschatology? Is it a theology of the future? Or, may it be better understood as a theology of the present? Are there other alternatives, relating present and future?

One writer[1] distinguishes five kinds of eschatology:

(1) *Consistent eschatology.* Jesus' eschatology was central, not peripheral to his thinking. Jesus and the first generation of Christians anticipated the end of history in *their generation*. It did not happen. So eschatology has been nullified as history moved on. Proponents: J. Weiss, A. Schweitzer.

(2) *Realised eschatology.* Jesus was actually introducing the kingdom not simply announcing what was going to happen. The end was fully realised with the coming of Christ. *Luke* 17:21: 'The Kingdom of God is in the midst of you.' Proponent: C. H. Dodd.

(3) *Heilsgschichte eschatology.* This combines the future and present aspects of Jesus' teaching of tension between the

---
1 Carl E. Braaten, *History and Hermeneutics*. Philadelphia: The Westminster Press, 1966, chapter 6, pp. 160-174.

'already' and the 'not yet.' We recall the past and anticipate the future of Christ's coming. Proponent: Oscar Cullman, *Christ and Time*.

(4) *Existentialist eschatology* is not futuristic, but concerns the present possibilities of human existence. Eschatology is contemporised. Fulfilment is now. Proponent: Rudolph Bultmann.

(5) *Dialectical eschatology*. There is a dialectical relation between time and eternity. Eternity breaks into the earthly and human. The 'last' things are the 'ultimate things' of life. The question is, How are time and eternity related? The stress is on the idea that the present is the bearer of eternal meaning.

Other writers distinguish other types.[1]

The idea of eschatology has become a major concept in the vocabulary of contemporary theology. It is being employed in the service of quite different approaches to the expression of Christian faith. It has opened up new possibilities for thinking in a range of theological disciplines, for example in New Testament Studies and philosophical theology. The distinctive Christian Scriptures are to be viewed as eschatological and the central figures Jesus and John the Baptist in the Gospels as eschatological prophets. In the work of Jürgen Moltmann, eschatological ideas form an essential role

---

1 e.g. Hans Conzelmann, *An Outline of the Theology of the New Testament*. London: S. C. M. Press, 1969, p. 308.

(1) Thoroughgoing eschatology: Since the *parousia* did not materialise 'the church was forced to establish itself in the world by reflection and organisation.'

(2) Realised eschatology (C. H. Dodd): futuristic eschatology is a secondary stage. God's Kingdom came into the world with the coming of Jesus.

(3) Salvation-history interpretation of the New Testament. (O. Cullmann and others.)

in the development of philosophical and political ideas within a theology of history.

Eschatology Future

John Milton in his epic poem, *Paradise Lost,* imagined a great cosmic conflict. It began in the aeons before the creation of our universe. It involved supernatural creatures, organised within a hierarchical structure. Lucifer the archangel rebelled against the Almighty and was cast out of heaven to dwell in hell. But with the creation, he brought sin and death into the newly formed world and waged bitter warfare against the Almighty and his creatures. He continues to wreak evil, causing the death of Jesus and continuing his work even now only, so the epic goes, until the last conflict when in the final battle he will succumb to the power of God and be ultimately destroyed in the Lake of Fire.

This is the stuff of apocalyptic writing. We read the same epic story in the book of *Revelation*, where the supernatural forces of good and evil meet in continual encounter. The final outcome, that which constitutes the *eschaton*, takes place when the Devil, Satan, his angels, and those whom he has persuaded to evil are judged and ultimately destroyed. Peace finally reigns throughout the universe and the purpose for creation is ultimately achieved.

How is this system achieved? It is the result of quite simply collating passages from the book of *Revelation* while interpreting the symbols and referring the application to the future. This produces a sequence of events. Some passages are taken literally, for example the period of the thousand years, and the great ultimate battle when Satan will try to take the New Jerusalem but be defeated and cast into the abyss.

Since this writing is providing an introduction to contemporary discussions of eschatology, its assumptions, methods and results, it is quite appropriate that we include an account of views held by many conservative Christians. So in the following we shall attempt two tasks: (1) To state the assumptions the conservative

Christian makes. (2) to give an account of a resulting eschatological scheme which may be taken as representative.

To find a contemporary example of this eschatological scheme, and peruse it in some detail we go to Adventist teaching. The source is the book *The Great Controversy between Christ and Satan*. In it we get an exposition of a lengthy, elaborate and detailed series of supernatural events, taking place in the 'heavens' and culminating with the coming into being of the New Earth and the establishment of the New Jerusalem and the eternal life of the blessed redeemed, who have been duly translated or resurrected. To this end the Adventist Christian looks eagerly forward. At almost every funeral service the certainty is expressed that at the last day the deceased will live in heaven and be reunited with the mourners after they in due course become the deceased. That this prophetic system is truly a monumental achievement will become apparent from a detailed summary.

Sometimes, perhaps when we are not thinking about it, we do not recognise that we are making assumptions. If and when we start to think we may do, and then either question them or take them for granted, as if not open to or not needing examination, for example about the millennium. It is not our purpose here to question these assumptions. We shall simply state them, so as to make explicit the shared assumptions of the believer in the soon return of Jesus. We may then examine the belief in the imminent *parousia* held within the context of these assumptions.

Basic Assumptions

God acts within the world to fulfil his will.

Jesus after the ascension is alive and is living in the heavens.

Jesus is aware of and living in relation to a space-time related to our space-time

Jesus shares our experience so that it is possible for him to appear in a form which we will recognise.

In due course Jesus will move from the space-time in which he dwells and break into our space time.

This 'coming' = '*parousia*' = 'advent' will mark the beginning of events which introduce the after life.

Jesus, the agent of God's action, will return to the earth in which he once lived and died to bring the will of God to final fulfilment.

This involves the judgement and destruction of evil along with the restoration of the earth to become the home of the blessed good, i.e. heaven for ever.

Jesus is the central figure in the renewed earth.

Assumptions concerning Scripture

Scripture is to be literally interpreted.

The author of the writing is the one whose name is featured in the writing.

The date of the writing is determined by reference to the one whose name is featured in the writing.

Words attributed to Jesus are those actually spoken by Jesus. This is clear from the production of red letter Gospels, in which words associated with Jesus are printed in red.

What the Gospels say Jesus said and did, Jesus said and did.

Because Scripture is God-given and so inspired, it has unquestionable authority. This authority is called into question if the text is not taken for what it says.

Everything that can be taken as literal is to be taken literally. So terms are to be given a literalist meaning, as closely as is possible to the original. Miracle stories are accounts of actual events. Fire is actual fire. The Millennium is actually a thousand year period of our time.

We then can work out a sequence with a human time scheme. The millennium becomes one thousand literal years, or is asserted without much thought as to the implications of taking it in terms of its actual temporal reference. When taken literally, it is at least twelve times a reasonably lengthy human life span.

Assumptions concerning Prophecy and the End

Prophecy (including apocalyptic) is history in advance, often presented in symbols.

Symbols are to be interpreted by reference to events in the future: some historical, some trans-historical.

Numerical references are to be interpreted, i.e. deciphered, by reference to particular historical events, periods, persons, and organisations. This is to be accomplished where time is concerned by employing the year for a day principle, i.e. a day in the text stands for a year in actual time.

Assumptions concerning an Imminent Second Advent

Long-term predictions have not yet been fulfilled..

When saying that the Advent is 'soon' (or when using synonyms), we may not specify either the time of the coming, nor may we set a limit to the length of the intervening time, 'Soon' is extensible.

The Advent believed to be imminent has nevertheless been delayed.

The delay can be justified by understanding certain Scriptural passages.

Assumptions concerning Eternal Life

How can we conceive what the *parousia* introduces, when time is taken up into eternity? Conservative hopes are often dissatisfied with the confession that the content of the hope of eternal life, or even of everlasting life, is to be left in God's hands. They require some descriptive content to be given to that which transcends all our ideas. They take the symbolic language of the Apocalypse, for example, as providing real descriptions. They carry over the temporal sequence of our space-time into the realm beyond the *parousia*, the transcendental realm. Heaven is described to be very much like our current existence, but with everything removed that is inharmonious and hurtful. Heaven is not beyond time, beyond

Eschatology

knowledge. Attempted descriptions of everlasting existence in some writers who venture into the unknown make it very much like a kind of enhancement of what is desirable to human life. For example, pictures in the book of *Revelation* of rivers, gates, are to be taken literally. Fruit trees are real trees. Streets are literally golden. Gates are literally pearly. The blessed are in the presence of Jesus who is available to each one as friend and as object of reverence.

The negative aspect of these assumptions is that they lead to opposition to the liberal and critical theologians and literary critics. 'Criticism' is a negative concept, in whatever form it appears. As such it is to be rejected as harmful.

An Example

In what follows we have an illustration of a literalistic interpretation of a futurist eschatology. It is one worked out in very great detail, more detailed than others of like approach. The approach follows certain rules of method: First: Scripture supplies the content. There must be verses of Scripture to support the point of departure and the content. Second: Symbols mean literal events. Third: the one thousand years are literal and so are to be measured in earth time.

We now make a brief examination of this clear statement of literalistic eschatology which may be taken as a personal understanding of the author, and as official belief of the community, expressed in the book *The Great Controversy*. (The numbers in the following text are page references.) Within the Adventist community this personal understanding of the last things is taken as an authoritative predictive description of literal events at the end.

The theme of the book is that there is a seven thousand year exhibition of the controversy between Christ and Satan after the creation. The Miltonic contest, at first in the heavens, is carried over into the newly created earth where Satan has persuaded multitudes to rebel against their creator, by breaching the laws the creator gave to the human race. It is then finally completed in the trans-worldly sphere. What now follows is a brief summary of the book's portrayal of the course of events at the end.

Jesus descends in majesty to the mount of Olives as the righteous dead are resurrected, while the wicked living are destroyed. This is the first resurrection. The living 'righteous' are transformed and removed from a devastated earth. Here Satan remains alone, confined, a prisoner.

The millennium begins. The righteous have been taken to the City of God (647) Much detail is here supplied. It is the time of judgement. During the thousand years the righteous examine the records that have been kept of the wicked. These are preserved in books (666). These have been separated from the books recording the deeds and thoughts of the righteous. Their status has been decided after the 'investigative judgement' had run its course. That process began in A. D. 1844, and was completed before the Second Advent. We hear nothing of these records.

The millennium comes to an end. After the examination of the evidence comes the execution of the final judgement. The wicked are now raised to life, and Satan, who has been bound to a desolate earth, is brought to be with the resurrected wicked. They are made to see the spectacle of their deeds and the sufferings they have caused, not least the suffering of Jesus. Then the sentence of eternal death is pronounced upon them (668).

Satan rallies them all for a last final assault against the Creator, even after he has acknowledged the justice of God's judgement. The host of the wicked led by Satan attempt to storm the New Jerusalem. This final revolt fails. The wicked then meet their punishment which is in each case commensurate with the extent of their wickedness, some suffering longer than others. Satan suffers the most. They are made to suffer before they finally die. The final death, the 'second death', follows.

Eternity begins for the righteous.

Observations

What seems to be assumed in these descriptions, and we have here only provided a sample, is that the transcendent can be adequately described in the limited vocabulary of the human and the descriptions are to be taken literally. Paul had warned against this when saying that human emotions and concepts were quite inadequate; 'eye hath not seen, nor ear heard . . . .' (*I Corinthians 2:9*).

The time scale of the Millennium is literal. These years are a thousand of our years. The process of judgement is literal. The sentence is literal suffering. The preliminary selection of the righteous has already literally taken place. There are literally books of record. There has been a continuous process of recording deeds and thoughts in the books of record during the preceding 'six thousand years' of human life on earth. These accounts are the product of angelic activity continuous with every human life moment by moment.

What is also assumed is that God must demonstrate that he has been just in his judgements. There must be a rational justification of his decisions. It is not enough that the righteous simply be presented with the gift of eternal life, but they must be involved in the process of examination of the ones God rejects and by being so involved be convinced of his justice. However they do not have executive authority. They are permitted, indeed enjoined, to examine the records of the activity of beings whose fate has already been decided and the decision already acted upon. After all they are now already dead. So the Millennium is a lengthy time of providing vindication for judgement already executed. It ends with the rational acknowledgement of God's justice. The task of such extensive examination over such an extended period is demanded of the righteous, imposed upon them. We seem to be a very long way away from the experience of trust and faith in God as Protestants have understood it.

Your job, if you make it to be among the righteous at the first resurrection, will be to spend 1000 times 365 days in the process of judgement. Simply to think of the notion, let alone contemplate the prospect of the activity, boggles the mind. Even accepting the assumptions and allowing the possibility of such descriptions, can one view the account as intelligible, let alone credible? Since a year is a measurement of the length of time for the earth's rotation around the sun. But the righteous are not on the earth, but in the New Jerusalem which has not yet descended to the earth.

Existentialist Eschatology Celebrating the Present

New Self-understanding.

After his death, Jesus is proclaimed as 'the eschatological event'. The proclamation however and whenever it occurs results in the faith of the believer. That faith is the experience of a new understanding of the self and of its possibilities, one which is quite contrary to the self-understanding of modern man. This new self-understanding, resulting from the human decision, constitutes a new person. The transformation of the understanding is so radical that it is described as the eschatological event. So Bultmann wrote:

'If men are standing in the crisis of decision and if precisely this crisis is the essential characteristic of their humanity, then every hour is the last hour. . . .'[1]

The New Testament expresses this in symbolic terms and in the context of an understanding of the world we no longer can share, the universe as 'three-storied': flat earth, heaven above, underworld beneath, the supernatural having access to the natural and human. This mythological eschatology is untenable for the simple reason that the *parousia* of Christ never took place as the New Testament expected.[2]

---

1   Rudolf Bultmann, *Jesus and the Word.* New York: Charles Scribner's Sons, 1958, p. 52.
2   Rudolf Bultmann, (Hans Werner Bartsch (editor), Reginald H. Fuller translator). 'New Testament and Mythology' in *Kerygma and Myth,* London: S. P. C .K. p. 5.

Eschatology

These then are the two strands of Bultmann's reconstruction of eschatology: (1) contemporary man's understanding of himself and of the universe in which he lives are in direct opposition to those of the New Testament. (2) The *parousia* did not take place as the New Testament expected.

So a reconstruction of the understanding of Christian faith must take place. Such faith comes to be in the present. The whole stress is on the contemporary happening of the Word, on the effectiveness in the present of the proclamation, the *kerygma*. The proclamation is of Jesus, 'Jesus is risen'. The result of this proclamation is the event of faith, the emergence of the new self-understanding. This is not the product of the human will, but the effect of the revelation of God through the proclamation of Jesus. The questions now arise, 'What if any is the connection of such proclamation to the historical Jesus? Is the eschatological being set in opposition to the historical?'[1] Bultmann believed that this interpretation preserves the Lutheran stress on the principle of *sola fide,* justification by faith alone. Historical knowledge cannot serve as a basis for faith. Salvation does not depend on knowledge. That is Gnosticism.

---

1 This equates history with meaning. e.g. Carl Michalson, *The Rationality of Faith.* London: S. C. M. Press, 1964, p. 62 '. . . history is meaning and not fact. . . .' The meaning of the resurrection of Jesus is about the future. 'In the resurrection Jesus ascends to the Father. The Father of Jesus is God. Henceforth his father will be our father. That is the meaning of the resurrection. . . . (*John* 20:17).' p. 52.

In opposition to a view which equates history with meaning is the view that 'History is not synonymous with time or the self-consciousness: 'history' includes the impact of events, but not in isolation from those events as objective happenings.' Philip Hefner, *Faith and the Vitalities of History,* pp. 130-131. So Bultmann's eschatology is vacuous. Cf. Robert W. Jenson, *Systematic Theology,* Volume I. Oxford, University Press, 1997, pp. 171, 173: 'What must be recovered, precisely within the Bultmannian problematic, is the old and material answer: a future determined as fellowship with Jesus.'

Realised Eschatology

C. H. Dodd was exercised over the question of the relation between history and eschatology. History can be reported if past, and can be predicted if future i.e. what will be history when the future becomes past. Events are established by evidence. When and if they happen as predicted, they can be related to the predictions that anticipated them. A simple but basic point is that the term 'historical' refers to events that happen within the cosmos while the term 'eschatological' has reference to events outside of history. The term 'eschatological' points to reality beyond human experience and beyond human comprehension. Historical events can be reported if past and can be predicted if future. The event established by evidence may then be related to the prediction. On these definitions the question arises as to whether future historical events accompany or anticipate eschatological. Can we move from the prediction of the historical event to the occurrence of the eschatological? Is the destruction of Jerusalem both a prediction of a historical and a symbol of the transcendent end-event?

What is the relation between what Jesus believed and taught and the belief and teaching of the early church? What Jesus actually taught is to be established by historical inquiry. Dodd says, '. . . the thought of Jesus passed directly from the immediate situation to the eternal order lying beyond all history of which He spoke in the language of apocalyptic symbolism.'[1] With the coming of Jesus crisis has entered the world. So decision and watchfulness are demanded by that event.

This was a common theme between Jesus and the early church: the exhortation to watchfulness. In Jesus' day, it was because with him the Kingdom had broken in to history and his hearers had to be aware and to be decisive. In *Luke* as in *1 Thessalonians* the eschatological motif is introduced to the general teaching about being

---

1 C. H. Dodd, *The Parables of the Kingdom*, p. 154.

awake. 'the reason for "watchfulness" is the certain approach, and the uncertain date, of the second advent of Christ'[1]

The *eschaton* had come with the coming of Jesus. The second coming would soon take place and the age would end. The anticipated event did not occur as expected. The first Christians had to come to terms with the situation. This was the context for the development of early Christian thought.

The Salvation-Historical Interpretation

This approach stands in contrast to the existentialist interpretation of eschatology. It is exemplified in the writings of Oscar Cullmann who persistently engaged in a running debate with Rudolph Bultmann. His earlier book *Christ and Time* had met with heavy criticisms. His later book *Salvation in History*[2] was an attempt to answer explicit criticisms and to clarify his position

If the tension between the 'already' and the 'not yet' in the New Testament and in the Christian message is maintained, there is no antagonism between 'salvation-history' and Christian existentialism. Indeed the two positions are complementary. To raise the essential question of continuity between the historical Jesus and the Christ of faith is to press beyond the position of Bultmann. The question is whether a sequence of events can be an object of faith as well as of assent. Cullmann answers with an emphatic affirmative. In faith the believer is overwhelmed by that in which he did not participate (p. 115). The events of salvation are *pro nobis*, but first they are *extra nos*.

In contending for the priority of salvation-history over revelation, the polemic is directed against Pannenberg, who according to Cullmann, subordinates salvation to revelation. We must press back behind the process of interpretation to get at the events. The historical must be separated from the interpretative and the mythological if we want to see how revelation occurs in history. The

---

1 *Ibid.,* pp. 117-118.
2 Oscar Cullmann, *Salvation in History.* References in the text are to this book.

interpretation must come from the events themselves, 'out of the naked events' (p. 96). This is repeatedly emphasized by Cullmann.

There is, however, a relationship to the facts that is independent of faith, a preliminary hearing (p. 71). There is a sequence of events which can be unfolded as history quite independent of whether the faith-encounter ensues or not. But when faith is present there is to the believer a coincidence of the historical and the theological (p. 71). Before this coincidence there must be the *Vorverständnis* (pre-understanding) of the acceptance of the objective reality of 'a series of divine events.' The discernment of this crucial sequence of events, selected out of history as such, is what constitutes faith. To the historian the sequence upon which faith depends is quite meaningless. Proper interpretation of the events is disclosed in and with the events themselves. The supreme example of this is the resurrection of Jesus (pp. 102-123), where we are given the paradigmatic case of the coincidence and simultaneity of event and interpretation. Here the divine event is known through a proper interpretation of historically accessible facts, open to alternative interpretations. The essential ingredient of salvation-history, that which constitutes an event a 'divine event,' is beyond the range of historical knowledge. Thus there is a fundamental, a priori distinction between historical knowledge and salvation-historical knowledge of a divine event (p. 151). Eschatological considerations are worked out from this viewpoint.

The decisive events *extra nos* at the basis of the Christian faith constitute the mid-point of time. What is essential at the mid-point must come to its expression at the end. The eschatological consummation expresses the meaning of all history. 'Light from the eschaton falls back upon the central portion of history' (p. 147). Thus the *eschaton* is anticipated in the central happenings of the Christ-event. It is both present and future.

Important Questions

As we approach the subject of eschatology there are important questions we have to answer before we can proceed. One of the most important has to do with what I can believe. It is crucial to be very clear about the answer you give to this basic question. The reason is that it will influence how you resolve some of the issues we are raising. So put bluntly, Ask and give a candid answer to the questions:

What can I believe and what can I not believe? What are the implications of the answers I give to the question? This question then ramifies into more precise formulations.

What can I not believe about how things happen in the system of an ordered cosmos?

What can I not believe about how historical reports come to be written?

What can I not believe about the reliability of human testimony as an avenue to knowledge, whether given verbally or in writing?

What can I not believe about the capacity of a being with human limitations to foretell the future?

What can I not believe about the supernatural?

What can I not believe about claims that the supernatural causes events to take place within the cosmos?

Natural events have natural causes. That is the principle we take for granted. It constitutes the empirical assumption we make in all of our everyday and scientific activity. It provides the criterion for and sets a limit to our knowledge. We do not accept as possible knowledge what does not fit with this principle. We test claims about past, present and future by applying it. We assess the status and intent of a document as we apply the principle to its content. We make judgements about the reliability of reports and testimony by applying this principle to what they report. This also involves judgements about the writers or speakers whose reports we are assessing. If they present as fact what we consider impossible, we first question their purpose. We assess their credibility, trustworthiness and integrity as we discern whether they adhere to the principle.

Traditional Christian faith is based on a supernaturalistic metaphysics. That faith claims that the Scriptures are supernaturally inspired. The events of the Bible are the product of the supernatural incursion of God into history. The events basic to the emergence of Christianity are unique. The Gospels provide an authentic literal account of the events and sayings ascribed to Jesus and of what happened to him. This understanding began with the present faith of the believer.

So it is important that we consider, assess and make a judgement about the following assertion. To believe that events occurred on the basis of faith, to attach faith to historical claims is to pervert historical judgement by repudiating the basic empirical principle. This requires that historical claims are established by evidence For the historian all historical claims are probable. All historical sources are to be assessed for their evidential value. They are to be assessed and not taken for granted as authentic and authoritative in themselves. The historical sources, in this case the Gospels, are to be assessed according to the principles of historical method.

DISCUSSION QUESTIONS
Chapter 6

(1) What is dualism? Why did the early church reject dualism as taught for example by the Gnostics?

(2) Is John Milton's epic conflict, *Paradise Lost,* dualistic? What meaning do you give to the story of a supernatural conflict between ultimate powers?

(3) We cannot construct a theology without making assumptions. With what assumptions would you organise your beliefs? Which of the assumptions suggested in the chapter would you be in agreement, and which would you reject?

(4) The Christian finds meaning for his present life in considering the eschatology of the New Testament. So Christian eschatology can be thought of as self-understanding transformed by the contemplation of Jesus Christ and the New Testament *kerygma*.

Is that sufficient?

(5) Review the section *Important Questions* and give your own answers to them. Also give reasons for your acceptance or rejection.

7

Resurrection

Life After Death?

The hope of resurrection, the belief of many Christians, is clearly expressed in the scriptural words set to music in Handel's Messiah.

'The trumpet shall sound, and the dead shall be raised incorruptible, and we shall be changed. For this corruptible must put on incorruption, and this mortal must put on immortality.'[1]

It is clearly expressed in the final words of the Apostles' Creed:

'(I believe in) the resurrection of the body and the life everlasting. Amen.'

It is repeated in similar words in the Nicene creed:

'I look for the resurrection of the dead, and the life of the world to come. Amen.'

The end of human existence would not in itself be a victory of good over evil. We can contemplate the total destruction of human life with horror and regret because we cannot be certain that, now that it is within human power to bring about, we shall not with some future act of madness initiate such annihilation of our own human accord.

Eschatological thought has always insisted that we come to terms with the possibility of the continuance of human life after

---

1 The words are part of the passage in *I Corinthians* 15: 51-54.

death. It has expressed this hope in two ways in addressing the question of how such continuance will come about: through the idea of the immortality of the soul, and through the idea of resurrection.[1] We discuss the latter here.

What is the content of this hope of a literal resurrection of the body after death at the end? It is that there is resuscitation of 'body'. Does that mean that there is a revival of the person? Will the being that results be the same person who previously existed, however changed the conditions? Will that being be continuous with the earthly creature? The philosophically inclined will discuss the meaning of personal identity and, if theologically inclined as well, apply the conclusions to address the question about survival post mortem.

Is the question of post mortem existence a rational question? Does it have any empirical connection? It is now a hope. Could it be that we can move from hope to knowledge? The only way we could know whether the hope is sustainable is when we experience its fulfilment. By then it is rather late! If we experience resurrection we shall know. If we do not, we shall never know.[2] Obviously that

---

1 We shall not elaborate on the idea of the immortality of the soul here. The existence of the soul as a component of the human person is a part of Christian tradition but is an unfortunate error. Cf. E. W. H. Vick, *Death, Immortality and Resurrection* for a succinct theological and philosophical treatment.

2 This line of thought has come to be called 'eschatological verification'. The point is that the sentence predicting resurrection, 'The dead will be raised' is a statement. That is to say it makes a claim that can be empirically verified. Since it is a claim about the future, that verification will be future. It will consist in the event taking place. Falsification means the showing of a claim to be false. That is also an empirical condition for a sentence to be cognitively meaningful. In the case of final resurrection, verification is available. But falsification is not. We shall never know if the claim is false. I shall never know that the claim 'you will be resurrected' is false since I shall not be resurrected to know. The application of a similar argument to our present is also relevant. We only believe in resurrection if we can cite one example of resurrection experienced and confirmed. Failing that, sentences about resurrection are not statements, and cannot be considered as assertions, claims.

Eschatology

does not give us the grounding we want in the present, but leaves us with a theoretical possibility.

We had earlier on talked about the ambiguity of words and the misconstruing of meaning that sometimes results when two parties attempt communication. The term 'resurrection' provides us with an example. The creed speaks of the 'resurrection of the body'. The expression here stands for the bringing into being again of a living person. The dead has been given new life.

What is interesting is that Paul uses both the terms 'dead' and 'resurrection' in two different senses. He relies on an analogy between the two meanings to give plausibility to a metaphorical use of the terms. Before faith one is dead, 'dead in trespasses and sins'. With the coming of faith one lives, having been 'raised'. The symbolism of baptism serves to suggest emergence of a new life, a new being. Having been immersed in the water you rise up to a new life. That is resurrection in its second and derived sense: the coming to have faith, to be a new person, to have a new understanding of self and the world. That meaning of resurrection can become the basic meaning of the term.

So when you speak of the resurrection in connection with Jesus the Christ who has made possible a new life for the believer, and take this as the basic meaning of resurrection, you are making an assertion quite different from the other meaning that claims that a dead Jesus became a living Jesus, that the grave in which he was placed after death was empty because he had been bodily raised from the dead. Here it is used of the believer's experience of spiritual life flooding into the mundane existence, whether of the individual or of the community. It is equivalent to the coming of the Spirit, the experience of God's grace. That experience is so revolutionary and creative that it bears comparison to life restored after physical death. Paul speaks of becoming a 'new creation'. So it is appropriate to have the same term used of it as would be used if you had been a corpse and then had the experience of coming to a new life. So Paul associates it with baptism which he uses as a symbol of the experience. You rise from the water a new person. Paul found no problem in using the term in both senses of the real future hope of bodily change and of the experience of coming to Christian faith. If resurrection did not signify the literal coming to life again the analogy would, for Paul, lose its content.

For a very long time, under the influence of Plato, Christians believed the soul to be immortal, that the soul was the essential element in the human person, and that the soul survived the dissolution of the body. That is to say, the soul is inherently immortal. That being so, it survives death. Plato produces an elegant argument for this position. If the human person is composed of body and soul, and the soul is immortal and the essence of the person, then deathless existence is entailed. Plato endorsed and argued for this conviction. Death means the separation of the soul from the body, its emancipation from all that in this life restricted and fettered it.[1]

For Plato life after death is assured because of what the human being essentially is. But some Christians have denied this. The reason is that it leaves the action of God out. 'We believe in the life to come, not because man is what he is, but because God is what he is.'[2] The hope of eternal life is not based upon the nature of the human soul as such, but upon a relation which exists or may exist between the human soul and God.[3]

Resurrection of Jesus and Final Resurrection

Resurrection and History

In English there is one word for history, the word 'history.' In German there are two words: *Historie* and *Geschichte*. They are synonyms. But since there are two different words, a distinct mean-

---

1 Plato, *Phaedo*, 67-68. B. Jowett (translator), *The Dialogues of Plato, Volume 1*. New York: Random House, 1937, pp. 450-451.
2 John Burnaby, *The Belief of Christendom*. London: S. P. C .K., p.192. 'The hope of eternal life is not based upon the nature of the human soul as such, but upon a relation which exists or may exist between the human soul and God.
3 Oliver C. Quick *Doctrines of the Creed*. London: Collins, 1968, p. 264.

Eschatology

ing can be given to each. Theologians have taken advantage of this and have given different meanings to each, making the distinction between an objective and a subjective meaning. *Historie* has reference to those events that take place in space and time outside the consciousness of the individual. *Geschichte* has reference to events that take place within the consciousness either of the individual or of a community.

The issue with which we are concerned is over the meaning of resurrection. The question is what sort of event the resurrection of Jesus is. That means asking whether historical evidence can establish it, whether such appeal is even possible, i.e. whether it is an historical event on a par with all other historical events. To speak of it as a 'sort of event' is already to invite confusion. Here a crucial division takes place between opinions. The division results in different theologies. We distinguish three approaches.

(1) One firmly denies physical resurrection and, operating with two different senses of the term 'history', reinterprets the event in terms of the believer's experience.

'So far as it is an event that God causes to occur to the pre-existent son of God, it seems to take place in a mythical sphere outside the realm of human experience. . . . For the resurrection, of course, simply cannot be a visible fact in the realm of human history.' Appeal to witnesses by Paul in view of Gnostic objections is therefore not convincing.[1]

(2) Others attempt to recognise the possibility of historical verification, again operating with different senses of the term 'history'.

While earlier he denied that the resurrection was an historical event, i.e. one accessible to the historian, Karl Barth later modified that view. He then questioned that

---

1 Rudolph Bultmann, *Theology of the New Testament, Volume I.* London: S. C. M. Press, 1956, p. 295.

the modern world-view should have the final word in assessing the biblical narratives of the resurrection of Jesus.

'We must still accept the resurrection of Jesus, and His subsequent appearances to His disciples, as genuine history in its own particular time ... the narratives are not meant to be taken as "history" in our sense of the word ... they are describing an event beyond the reach of historical research or depiction.' The narratives are not myth, but 'couched in the imaginative, poetic style of historical saga and are therefore marked by the corresponding obscurity'.[1]

One line in recent thought about the problem of resurrection and history makes the suggestion that, since we are dealing with trans-human realities in speaking of resurrection, only with the break-in of the new reality will we have a context in which we shall be able to understand Jesus' resurrection. What happened at the resurrection of Jesus can only be understood with the event of the parousia.

Pannenberg suggests that only with the break-in of the new reality will we have a context in which we shall be able to understand Jesus' resurrection. Then we shall have evidence which is at the present unavailable because beyond our ability to know. or ascertain. He writes:

'The description of the event (the resurrection of Jesus) in the language of the eschatological hope still proves itself to be the most plausible, in the face of all rival explanations.'

'The historian's judgement is often determined and limited from the outset by his previous understanding as to the orbit of possibility.... Can the historian

---

1 Karl Barth, *Church Dogmatics. Volume III, Part two.* Edinburgh: T. & T. Clark, 1960, pp. 447, 452.

reckon with the break-in of an end-time reality which does not take the same form as other historical events?'

'The general context of experience into which Jesus' resurrection can be fitted... will only be established through the eschatological consummation of all things . . . . The distance of the present world from the eschatological future of God does not exclude the real appearance of the future in our present world'. But 'this basic assertion of its faith will remain a matter of dispute in this world. But it is neither confuted, nor does it lack for evidence'.[1]

What this implies is that the reality is not readily accessible to the historian, making the assumptions he presently makes, but that the historian must adjust his understanding of reality so as to be able to understand and assess the resurrection of Jesus. To do this he must reckon with reality which does not present itself as do the historical events which are the historian's normal subject matter. However, the claim cannot be demonstrated and will always be a matter of dispute.

(3) The third firmly asserts not only the literalness of the resurrection of Jesus, but also that the New Testament provides sufficient evidence to establish its occurrence. New Testament statements are taken as authority for its literal occurrence. This means that the resurrection of Jesus can be made the subject of historical inquiry and judgement.

---

1 Wolfhart Pannenberg, *The Apostles' Creed in the Light of Today's Questions*. London: S. C. M. Press, 1972, pp. 113, 109, 114-115.

DISCUSSION QUESTIONS
Chapter 7

(1) What do you understand by the confession that Jesus rose from the dead?

(2) Was it an event that could have been witnessed? Or was it an event 'beyond the reach of historical research or depiction'?

8

Words And Meanings

Same Word, Different Meanings

One of the continual problems of communication and one which gives rise to much misunderstanding and sometimes even hostility, is that identical language can have very different meanings. I use a word as I understand it. You take the word I am using as you understand it and we go on talking until we discover that the same terminology has quite different senses for you than it has for me. Now you may not want to allow that my meaning is the right one. But if you are going to understand me, you may have to bracket your understanding and put your mind into my frame of reference. Or you can simply assert your meaning and reject mine. If you are enthusiastic and your conviction is unshakeable you may even become hostile. But without a mutual consideration the result is almost inevitably misunderstanding.

If I mean one thing by a term and you mean another, we shall have to see that difference and then we can either allow that both meanings are proper and recognise both usages. Or, if I use the term 'end' in one sense and you use it in another, it may be that neither of us will allow the propriety of the use the other is making. So there will be conflict, or without further consideration, rejection and possibly hostility. On the other hand you may see that one use of 'end' is different from the other and then understand why the term is used in that way. Then there can be mutual consideration and understanding.

There are some words that raise eyebrows and produce hostility when used in a certain context, simply by being heard, without further consideration given. In different contexts the same word may have a quite different status. One of these featuring in contemporary theological discussion is the word *myth*. It has not yet found ready acceptance with many a preacher and pew. We will now consider it briefly.

Myth

Let's start with a dictionary definition:

(1) 'A purely fictitious narrative involving supernatural persons, actions or events, and embodying some popular idea concerning natural or historical phenomena. Often used vaguely to include any narrative having fictitious elements.' *Shorter Oxford English Dictionary Volume II,* p. 1988.

The Greek myths are probably the most familiar.

(2) A non-scientific scheme for depicting the cosmos and a frame for setting events within it, for example, the pre-Copernican understanding of the universe, with flat earth, heavens above the earth, and the underworld beneath it. This is sometimes known as the three-storied universe. Various elaborations are possible within this schema. What is of interest to the contemporary theologian is this. It provided the ancient and the medieval for the depiction of natural events. The sun moved in the heavens. The earth was the centre of the universe. This was the framework within which supernatural events took place. Jesus went literally upwards into the heavens at the ascension. The myth that the universe was three storied (flat earth, heavens above, underworld beneath) provided the basis for the expression of traditional church doctrine, so stoutly defended by the ecclesiastical authorities who held doggedly to the geocentric universe. The church dogmas

demanded that man be at the centre of the universe. That claim involved that man's home, the earth, also be at the centre of the universe. The universe was geocentric. Giordano Bruno (1548-1560), and Galileo (1564-1641) got into serious trouble with the church authorities for suggesting that the universe was heliocentric.

What was once expressed in terms of myth is now expressed in empirical language. A frequent misunderstanding of the conservative Christian is that he thinks that when the term 'myth' is being used, the accounts of Scripture are being rejected in toto, that its authority is being undermined. But that is a serious misunderstanding. The irony is that those who sometimes quite vociferously repudiate the term know full well that they cannot and do not accept the pre-Copernican understanding of the universe. They do not then go on to ask the question, 'What, without taking the framework of a three storied universe a given, shall we now make of writings taking it for granted? What meanings do they offer us within this framework?' Failure to understand is sometimes accompanied by unintentional dishonesty (or is it self-deception?).

(3) Beside referring to the understanding of the structure of the universe, there is a further meaning in the religious and theological context. It here refers to the ideas that express the conviction that the supernatural causes events within the system of nature, the cosmos. Believers accept that such events occur, for example miracles or processes of healing inexplicable by presently known science. There are also the extraordinary natural events, tsunamis, earthquakes. These latter are explicable in scientific terms, but the believer sometimes takes the step of saying that God is their cause, claiming that God or God's agents

are responsible for such events. God either initiated such events or permitted them to happen. When such events are portrayed in Scripture, they are not fictions but actual happenings. Such divinely initiated events otherwise unexplained and apparently inexplicable provide the problem: What does it mean to say that the supernatural acts within the natural order? When angels talk to men, and stand in the way of the animal, when the sun stands still at the bidding of a warrior, when God causes the devastation of a hostile army, how does one explain the process?

The Creation story is presented within the context of the world-view we have outlined (2) above. It is also presented as the activity of superhuman and super-temporal divinity (3) above.

Soon

The term 'soon' is widely used in contexts referring to the end time. For the Apocalyptists the deliverance is near. For the early Christians the *parousia* will occur 'quickly'. For modern adventists, Jesus is coming again 'soon'. So it is appropriate that we give some consideration to the concept.

(1) Soon means 'in a short time', but since that phrase is a synonym for the word soon we really get no further unless in turn we say what a short time is. It is the same with any other synonym for soon. Soon means 'within a specific time not far off', whether the length is made explicit or implicitly understood. 'Soon' means 'within a limit', as in the example: 'He'll be here soon', where 'soon' means 'in half an hour but not longer than an hour'.

In the normal use of the term soon, we understand that there is a limit within which the term applies. In

Eschatology 81

our example it is one hour. We could designate this meaning of the word as soon-L. Read this as 'soon with an understood limit'.

(2) But what happens if you take the limit away and still insist on using the term? You have lost its cognitive meaning. You cannot look for evidence if you do not know what the claim precisely means. We might designate this use as soon-noL.

It is quite clear that there are two usages

Now apply this to our example, 'He'll be here soon.' and see what happens. The meaning of the sentence now changes radically. It will now mean something like: 'He'll be here in half an hour, or in an hour or in two hours or in a day or we don't know and can't specify when, but we hope it won't be long', *long* being the opposite of *soon*. It could be used to mean 'at any time in the future' while giving the impression that the speaker intends a much shorter time, a very much shorter time. So it could serve as the expression of a rather vague hope. But while vague hopes can give significance to human life, they cannot be logically established.

Obviously now the term has become so flexible that it loses its value as a pointer. Now apply these observations to the expression which interests us:

First, where a limit is set, say a hundred years, 'Jesus is coming again soon' means 'Jesus is coming in ten years, or twenty, but in not more than a hundred years.'

But on the second usage, where no limit is set, it comes to mean 'Jesus is coming at any time. We hope it will be soon in the first ordinary sense, but we don't know at all when, so we cannot hope definitely that it may be in that sense.' It is thus robbed of its capacity to specify and gets (in Luther's terms) a 'nose of wax' and becomes infinitely extensible. It has already been extended two thousand years in the history of the Christian church and getting on for two hundred in the Adventist church.

When asked for some clarification, Adventists will insist that they cannot say when or how long we are living before the Advent. It will be indefinitely soon. But that is literally nonsense. (This expression 'non-sense' is used here as a technical term.[1]) It leads to an impossible position by appearing to give a meaning to 'soon' which cannot be sustained. The future may be infinitely extensible if 'soon' has no restricting principle to give it reference. A limited future is defined by giving a specifiable date, or by proposing a specifiable limit to the time to elapse before the event. An infinitely extensible future contrasts to this. It is this qualification, 'We cannot specify a limit' that spells the death of the sentence as a statement. It's a case of death by a crucial qualification. Moreover, if the future is infinitely extensible, the urgency it hopes to suggest disappears and the term 'soon' becomes empty. It cannot then serve even as hortatory, as admonition.

The problem of misunderstanding arises because the meaning of the term 'soon' is obscured. The reason for this is that there is nothing to indicate that it is being used any differently than in its normal sense. We don't have a usage for the term 'soon minus limit' meaning 'sometime in the future within a period without limits.'

So misunderstanding can take place on two levels corresponding to the distinction we have made above.

You say, 'Margaret will go on holiday *soon.*' I may misunderstand your statement to mean 'in a couple of days', since I set the limit to 'within a week', whereas you know that she has had a long illness lasting years and is still recuperating. So you mean 'within a year'. When I understand the situation, I shall accept your definition.

The second kind of misunderstanding may occur when you tell me the end of the world is imminent, but have not set a limit to the reference of the word imminent. So, I understand it to mean

---

[1] 'Nonsense' is here used as a technical term. By 'sense' we refer to some kind of experience, typically seeing or hearing. By 'nonsense' we mean 'not within the range of human experience, neither verifiable nor falsifiable by human experience.' See the following chapter.

Eschatology

'within a decade'. But if, as has so often happened, it has not taken place within that time, and you nevertheless continue to make that statement, and go on making it decade after decade, unless you give me to understand a definite limit, your claim is empty, i.e. devoid of definite meaning.

But the confusion not only takes place between two persons or parties. It can occur in a single individual. So the mind is divided. 'Soon' normally means 'within a temporal limit'. But where the reference is to the end of the world the limit passes, not once but often, so it can't have meant that. So I must have misunderstood the meaning of the term. So I remove the limit that restricts the application of the term. I say to myself, 'It has not happened when I thought it would have forty years ago, thirty years ago, ten years ago. I now say, It will be soon, but I have no idea when.' But, since the non-limit use of the term renders it temporarily (with reference to passage of time) meaningless, I shall be confused. That seems inevitable. I want the term to mean 'within a restricted limit'. I also want it to be extensible when the event does not take place within the limit I have (tacitly or otherwise) in mind. My mind is divided. I am experiencing a kind of self-deception. I may not be up to reading the implications of my state of mind or I may not want to face the consequence of entertaining this double meaning. The situation is at any rate paradoxical.

That we set a limit to the application of the term 'soon' does not mean that the length of time to which we apply it may not vary, and vary considerably. The application of the word soon in different contexts can vary considerably. Within the limit that is set and understood the actual time expected may vary. But it will always vary within the limit.

Let's take some examples. Take the sentence, 'We shall know the result soon.' Now take different games. Soccer has two sessions of play, forty-five minutes each, so one and a half hours in total. 'We shall know the result soon' means, 'Within the limit of the two halves, which with the break amounts to an hour and three quarters.' Injury time has to be added to the total. Knowing this we may have to wait until the very last minute, so 'soon' has a limit then of two hours. But the claim, 'We shall know the result soon' could turn out to mean 'within twenty minutes' when we see one side so superior that it scored seven goals in the first half hour.

Test Cricket is a very different game. The length of time here is usually five days. You want to know the result of the match. Who will win? Will it be a draw? So 'soon' in the sentence in this context means 'at the most (i.e. within the limit of) five days'. But then Test matches are constituted by a series of several games, often five. So if at the beginning of the series we say that we shall know the result soon, that will mean 'as long as it takes within the series'. The series takes around two months. So the temporal limit for the reference of the term soon in this context would be two months. But again if one team wins two out of the first three matches and is doing very well on the third and you predict a win, that prediction will be fulfilled rather more quickly, well within the appropriate limit.

Let us take as a further example a project for the healing of a disease. The research has been going on for decades. But we can now anticipate its success 'soon'. The limit for the application of the term soon would in this case be longer, say ten years. If we speak of astronomical phenomena the temporal limit of soon could be extended to mean a few trillion aeons!

If the event of the *parousia* does not happen 'soon', i.e. within the vaguely conceived reference limit of the term 'soon', one still goes on saying 'soon'. For, even if one never discerns it, one has some idea of time limit — a contradiction of course! Just extend the reference of the term, stretch it out! It is this stretching that is the strange feature of this usage of the term. Keep using it, and keep extending the indeterminate reference, which it does not have! That is the point. It is without such specific reference, but I think I have some idea of what the word does not have!

No matter how long it will be in coming, the event will always be 'soon.' So you always start from 'now', not when the term 'soon' was first used. You never lengthen the time. You cannot because

Eschatology

you have not set a time! You just start from the present. The event is always said to be 'soon' provided that it has not yet happened.

Obviously, you can't do that for ever. How many times must you go on saying 'soon' till you realise you can't go on saying it any more?

Meaningless Sentences

In whatever context it appears, a sentence is cognitively meaningless[1] if it does not have a reference. It has to be tied to a point of reference. Otherwise it may have a non-referential meaning. But at the same time it will be empirically meaningless. This is the customary way we usually think.

Sentences which say the *eschaton* is near, imminent, soon, speedy are meaningless unless they specify a span of time between the present where the claim is purportedly being made and the event of the *eschaton*.

There are various contents and numerous such purported claims which do not fulfil this condition. They are meaningless and so cannot be either true or false. They are sometimes said to be 'nonsense'.[2]

Such are the claims of the apocalyptists who say the end is close, but give no further qualification. Such are also the claims of

---

1 A term is *cognitively meaningless* when there is no empirical evidence to verify or falsify it. 'I will come today' is a cognitive sentence, a statement. I am not playing with words, say with the word, 'day'. So you or anyone can witness to an event that shows the claim to be true or the non-occurrence which shows it to be false. 'I will soon spend time with you' is only a cognitive sentence, a statement, if evidence can be found for it, or against it. You understand it to mean, 'in a couple of days', but I am only saying 'soon' to make you happy and have no intention of coming at all. So the term has no reference for me, even if you give it one, and go on then to say, it was not true after your couple of days has come and gone. The sentence is not a statement, but you have taken it for one. Sad situation!

2 'Nonsense' is here used as a technical term. By 'sense' we refer to some kind of experience, typically seeing or hearing. By 'nonsense' we mean 'not within the range of human experience, neither verifiable nor falsifiable by human experience'. See the following chapter.

those, whatever else they say, who predict the imminent return of Jesus, the Second Advent, but make no further specification either as to the actual time or to the length of the intervening time within which limit the final event will take place.

DISCUSSION QUESTIONS
Chapter 8

(1) How can you avoid the negative response that the word 'myth' often engenders? Discuss the three possible meanings suggested in the text of this chapter. Which do you find appropriate in the context of Christian eschatology?

9

When 'Jesus Is Coming Again Soon' Cannot Be False

'Soon' Simple, 'Soon' in Depth

This chapter will have two parts.
The first will be in simple language.
The second will go into somewhat greater depth. So you can rest your eyes after reading the first part, and then move to the second more demanding part.
There is a glossary defining essential words at the end.

Part One

There are some sentences that cannot be false because they cannot be true either.
Why not?
What kind of sentence could that be? Does it depend on what the words mean or what even a single word in the sentence means, or on how the sentence is put together?
Take an example:
There was a farmer who had three sons. Each one of them said, 'Father, I shall come to help you soon.'
The first one, Bob, said 'I shall come to the farm soon, this Wednesday in fact.'

The second one, Tom, said 'I shall come to the farm soon, within the next ten days.'

The third one, Hank, said, 'I shall come soon, but I do not know when and cannot say when. Nor can I give you a set limit for when it will be.'

Father was well pleased, and went to bed content that evening.

The sons got together afterwards and fell into conversation. Hank said, 'Father seems very pleased and is looking forward to my help, even if I did not commit myself in any way. I did not give a particular date, and I did not set a time limit either.'

'So, what do you mean then? That is not a proper way to use the term "soon" is it? It amounts to an empty promise doesn't it?' asked Tom.

'I mean just what I said, I don't know when,' responded Hank.

Bob broke in, 'If you don't know when, then you cannot say 'soon' can you? Or if you do, it can't mean anything. We know what we mean. We know what we intend. Father knows exactly what to expect of us. But as far as you are concerned, you might as well not be coming to help at all. You have given Father hope by saying you will come soon. You have taken away all meaning by saying that "soon" does not mean what the rest of us take it to mean. It is an empty term.'

'So be it' said Hank.

'But look here,' exclaimed Tom. 'You have raised hopes in Father, but his hopes are not at all well founded.'

'Look!' said Hank, 'what is important is that dad is happy. I do not see myself in the near future being able to spare the time. But if Dad thinks and hopes that I shall be helping, that is what is important. Hank smiled and continued, 'Every time he asks why I have not yet come and when I will be coming I can always go on saying that I am coming soon to help. My "soon" is a kind of elastic "soon." It is an extensible "soon". So as long as Dad hopes and I go on saying I will come "soon", we are both happy. He is happy because he thinks I shall be not long in coming. I am happy not to have to fulfil a definite promise. My "soon" is a different "soon" from your "soon".'

'Promise!' shouted Will. 'You can't call that a promise when no-one can possibly know what it means in terms of real time. It can't be false and it can't be true. It's an empty sentence and such sentences can't be false or true.'

Bob said, 'We have given definite information about when he can expect us. You have not said anything at all. You could go on saying your 'soon' as long as you live!

So it was. Hank is still saying his 'soon' and Dad is still waiting expectantly.

Part Two

Sentences and Statements

If a sentence cannot be false, what is its status? What are the alternatives?

(1) The evidence for the truth of the statement is decisive.

(2) It is the kind of sentence that must be true. Logicians call this an *analytic statement.* Here are a couple of examples:

2 plus 2 equals four.
A door cannot be open and shut at the same time.

Such sentences are necessarily true by virtue of the meaning of the terms in them and the relation between them stated in the sentence.

(3) It is the kind of sentence that could not be either true or false. How can this be? There are various reasons. The definition of the terms, or the crucial term in the sentence make it impossible for there to be application of any evidence either to show it false or to show it true.

It is obvious that there are some sentences for which it is difficult to find a meaning. Nonsense sentences provide an example;
Grimbles are brilliant.

If such is really a nonsense sentence it cannot be either true or false. The reason is that a key term, in this case the subject, is meaningless. I cannot test the subject for meaning, since a grimble is a nonsense. So I cannot make any claim about this nonsense term.

Here we must make an important distinction for there are different kinds of meaning. Let us begin by talking about cognitive meaning. A sentence is cognitively meaningful if there is a state of affairs to verify it or to falsify it. If there is evidence to show it to be false then the statement is cognitively meaningful. Similarly if there is evidence to show that statement to be true it is cognitively meaningful.

The point is that a sentence is meaningful in this sense only if it can be verified or falsified. Not all sentences are like this. So we must make a distinction between a sentence and a statement. Not all sentences are statements. Some non-statements may imply statements.

'What a beautiful day!' is not a statement. It is an exclamation, and exclamations cannot be true or false. Mind you, they often imply states of affairs. But they are not statements of fact. Our sentence is not identical to 'Today is a beautiful day.' That is a claim. So it can be falsified.

We must therefore distinguish between sentences and statements.

Not all sentences are statements, i.e.
Some sentences are statements.
All statements are sentences.

Sometimes sentences that are statements are not intended to function simply to give information, but have the function of being exclamatory, emotive, hortatory.

Hortatory Meaning

Let's look at one example. Here is a sentence whose primary meaning is hortatory, even if it looks at first sight that it is stating simple facts:

It's six thirty and the shops shut at seven.

If you ask, 'What is the function of this sentence?' the answer might very well be that it is suggesting, urging, reminding you that you should be getting off to the shops. It is saying, 'Let's go. Hurry up!' That is a command and commands are not cognitive, i.e. they are neither true nor false. So the primary function of a sentence which makes a statement may not be to assert something, to inform you of a state of affairs, even if you take it to be doing that, but rather to arouse you to do something. Its primary function is hortatory. It may state a fact. But the statement of the fact is not the primary intended meaning of the sentence. Its primary meaning is non-cognitive. The essential function of such a sentence is not to state a fact, but by stating a fact to urge you to action:. Go and buy some bread while you can! Don't you know we're hungry?

Go back now to the sentence, 'Jesus is coming again soon.' If you believe that to be a statement and a true one, then it can also serve to urge you to action, give you comfort and courage, provide incentive to good works, etc. Indeed the one condition for this sentence to have such hortatory meaning is that you take it to be a statement and take the statement to be true. That is that you take 'soon' to have its ordinary meaning. The sentence can hardly inspire you to good works now if 'soon' means 'any time indefinitely in the future'. It has such appeal by creating a sense of urgency. That is a plausible response only if the time is brief, i.e. if 'soon' has its ordinary meaning. Only if the expected event is literally near at hand will the statement of the 'blessed hope' inspire you to piety and good deeds.

Here we can make an important point. I recall a question and answer session in which I was part of the panel responding to questions. Another member of the panel was holding fast to the traditional position on the nearness of the Advent. When pressed, to say what 'soon' meant his response was to provide synonyms for the term 'soon'. Jesus will come again 'in the near future'. But if synonyms retain the indefiniteness of the term 'soon' they cannot help. They simply repeat the indefiniteness of the original term. In the near future (but indefinite and with no limit set), imminent (but with no definite limit to the time involved) simply repeat the original obscurity. 'Near' and 'speedy' mean just the same as 'indefinite soon' when no limit is set for the reference of the terms.

Idiosyncratic Use of Language

So what is happening here? Such adventists give a unique meaning to the term 'soon', one that is not recognised. It means for them 'indefinitely soon'. That is unique, idiosyncratic.

We are reminded of Humpty Dumpty in *Alice in Wonderland*. He has been considering the idea of 'unbirthday' and advocates unbirthday presents. He approves of the following argument:

> There are 365 days in the year
> Only one of these can be a birthday.
> So there are 364 unbirthdays
> Therefore, there are 364 days when you might get un-birthday presents and only one for birthday presents.

He then exclaims, 'There's glory for you!' To this Alice replies 'I don't know what you mean by "glory".' Humpty Dumpty smiled contemptuously. 'Of course you don't — till I tell you. I mean "there's a nice knock-down argument for you!"' Alice objected. 'But "glory" doesn't mean "a nice knock-down argument."' 'When I use a word,' Humpty Dumpty said in rather a scornful tone, 'it means just what I choose it to mean — neither more nor less.' 'The question is,' said Alice, 'whether you can make words mean so many different things.' 'The question is,' said Humpty Dumpty, 'which is to be master — that's all.'

Alice would not have known how she was supposed to understand the word 'glory' if she had not been told by Humpty what he meant by it.

So let's suppose we pose a similar question: What do you mean by 'soon'? I would not know how I am to understand the word 'soon' unless you explain it to me. So I am told, When we use the term 'soon' it means 'in the indefinite future with no limit set. It's an indefinable 'soon'. It is an extensible 'soon'.

The big difference between the two cases is this. While Humpty's use is idiosyncratic, Humpty's term is given a clear sense. It could be used widely in that sense. Take it in that sense and his sentence is a claim. 'There's glory for you' is true. The argument is a valid argument. In contrast, an adventist's sentence with the meaning given to the term 'soon' is not capable of being either true or false.

'We do not set times' is a familiar claim of the adventist. That claim underwrites the seriousness with which no time limit is set as a matter of principle. Adventists have good reason to give for this principle. For it was by coming to terms with what came to be called the Great Disappointment that the Adventist church emerged into existence. That event was the consequence of setting a specific date for the Advent and so specifying in detail what 'soon' meant. But October 22, 1844 passed without the proposed and awaited Advent. It showed the claim to be a false one.

The principle was not always adhered to. Some Adventists believed that if you put the limit to the Advent far enough into the future you were safe in making a more definite prediction. 'There are those in this audience who will live to witness the Advent.' This claim was made and believed during and far into the interim period. Notice that 'soon' in our sentence taken with this time limit can be subject to test for truth or falsity. The decades passed and the statement has been shown to be false. It has also shown how precarious it is to make prophecies with a determinable time reference.

Ambiguous Language

The case of the term 'soon' is not one of simple ambiguity. In the case of ambiguity, readers or hearers must make up their minds how, i.e. in which of the two or more senses, the term is to be taken.

As an example, take the sentence 'I cannot stand any longer.' Is 'stand' to be taken literally? It then would mean, 'I am very weary. I have to sit down.' Or is it to be taken in another sense? 'I have had enough of your talk, thank-you very much!' What does the person at the other end of the telephone take it to mean when she hears the above sentence?

'My birds have all flown away!' says an ornithologist whose children have recently left home. That's easy enough to understand! Often it is not difficult to determine how a term, and so how a sentence is to be taken. That is because there is an general agreement that the term has more than one meaning. The context will then usually determine which one of the meanings this particular use has. But it is not always straightforward.

'Soon' is not an ambiguous term. It has a normal, accepted sense. There is no problem with its customary and legitimate use.

Take the case of a different kind, that of a sentence where a word or term is given a meaning it does not usually and readily have. What happens then? When a special meaning is given to a term normally understood in a different way, it is not so easy to avoid confusion, mistake or ignorance regarding what is being meant, and whether the sentence is cognitive or not i.e. whether it can be false, or true.

The initial response to such a sentence would be to read the word being used in a unique or subjectively defined sense as having its ordinary meaning and to interpret the sentence accordingly. So what, if you took the unique meaning of the term would be a cognitively meaningless sentence, is interpreted as a statement, i.e. a fact stating sentence.

Alice, remember, objects: 'But I do not use the word in that way!' and implies, 'Nor does anyone else except you.' If Alice can

Eschatology

say that, she has to interpret the term the creature is using in her familiar way. She then finds that if she does it makes no sense at all. Unless she is prepared to accept the sense Humpty Dumpty gives it, she will not understand what he means. But the last thing she expects is that the idiosyncratic use will become customary and normative. It will remain quite eccentric or only used by one creature, and perhaps understood by the few to whom he explains himself. The point is that if there is no equivalent in the language for the special use to which someone is putting the term, then misunderstanding, confusion or plain bafflement is bound to result. We shall return to this example later.

This is what happens with the sentence: 'Jesus is coming again *soon*' when a special use is being given to the term 'soon', a use that is to be found nowhere else in the English language.

Verification and Falsification

It is the case with some sentences that while it would be possible to verify them, it would never be possible to falsify them. We are here talking about sentences that refer to future events of a certain kind. How can statements about the future be either shown to be true or shown to be false? It is obvious that since predicted events are in the future, these events cannot be falsified or verified now, in the present. That can only take place in the future when their occurrence does or does not take place.

There are two conditions for such verification. The event must take place. There must be someone to experience or witness the event predicted. For examples:

1 *No one will survive the destruction of the universe and all living things.*

That is a statement. Since it makes a unique claim it **cannot be shown to be true.**

2 *After the Advent and the Judgement, the dead will be raised and all things will be renewed.*

That is a statement. It can be shown to be true. But it **cannot be shown to be false.**

There are two different sentences about the future which the adventist makes. These are

    1 Jesus will come again.

    2 Jesus will soon come again.

These separate into three, since 2 is ambiguous: 'Soon' has its normal meaning in 2a and is given a special meaning in 2b. We can spell these meanings out, and the different status which the two sentences have.

Let us start with 1 Jesus will come again. Is this a cognitive statement or a non-cognitive sentence? That is, can we provide empirical evidence of its truth or falsity? In contrast to sentence 2 Jesus will soon come again no reference is made in 1 to any time scale. So the question is, How shall we show it to be a fact, or show that it is not true, i.e. is not a fact?

The answer is interesting. The condition for its truth is that there be survivors who witness it. Since the resurrection of the dead is contained in the claim, then (if true) there will be witnesses. That is a possibility if it is (i.e. will be) true. Since that is a possibility, we can say that it is verifiable, i.e. can be shown to be true. But since there would be no survival if it is false, there would be no possibility of witness to its not having taken place. If it's true we shall know. If it's not true we will never know. Theologians have talked about 'eschatological verification'. This is what they have meant. If it is a true prediction we shall know. If it is not true we shall never know.

2a *Jesus will come again soon,* where **soon** means 'at a specifiable time, or 'within a specifiable limit'. So when they said, 'Millions now living will never die' that set a limit, say of (at the most) 130 years from the time it was said. It has been shown to be false.

2b *Jesus will come again soon,* where **soon** is unspecifiable, indeterminate and indeterminable. 'He will come soon but we have no idea when.' So there is no limit to the time span involved, whether you say it in A.D. 70, or in 1860, or in 2012, or at any later time, 'Soon' might mean 'in ten years', or 'in a hundred years' or 'in a thousand years' or 'whatever time it takes to whenever he comes'. We just cannot say.

Now we go on to ask, What is the status of this sentence with its use of the unusual sense of the word 'soon'? It is not a cognitive sentence. But when it is taken as such, as stating a true fact, it serves to express urgency, responsibility, need for appropriate action and, perhaps above all else, hope.

Summary

Some sentences cannot be false because they can be neither true nor false. They are non-cognitive, do not refer to a possible fact, are not open to falsification or verification because they do not have any reference to a state of affairs. Since the term 'soon' as here used is undefined and indefinite it is cognitively meaningless.

APPENDIX to Chapter 9

Neither true nor false Additional note In Summary Form

If a sentence cannot be false, does that mean that it must be true?

It seems a matter of common-sense logic to argue, If a sentence cannot be false, then it must be true. But to reason thus is to make a mistake. The reason is that it depends on why it cannot be false. Cases are different.

Case 1

A statement that is necessarily true cannot be false, and since it cannot be false it must be true. E.g., Two plus two is greater than 2 plus 1.

Case 2

A sentence that cannot be false sometimes has that status because it cannot be true either. A nonsense sentence would fall into this category: e.g. Miscongo has humprise. 'Twas brillig.'

If you allow that such nonsense words may be code, then the interpreted terms and sentences have a different status. You may then have rendered them into cognitive sentences. But you would have to know how to interpret them!

Case 3

A sentence with a qualifying term that is meaningless

The example of this article is that of 'soon'. I can qualify this term in such a way as to render it meaningless and a meaningless sentence can be neither true nor false. That means that the fact that it is not false does not mean that it has to be true. It may give the appearance of being an ordinary cognitive statement, but the crucial qualification renders the term without meaning and so renders the sentence in which it stands also cognitively meaningless.

Why a single qualification makes all the difference.

I have received a message: 'We will phone you soon.' But I am a busy person and do not want to hang around the phone waiting needlessly. So I ask for a qualification. 'When you say 'soon' what do you mean? When can I expect your call?' I get one of three answers:

1. at three o'clock this afternoon
2. within twenty-four hours
3. we do not know and cannot say

What would my response be to each of these answers?

To 1 I will answer: 'Thank you, I understand precisely.'

To 2 I will answer: 'Thank you. While I would have liked to know precisely, I shall expect your call in the knowledge that it will be soon.'

To 3 I will answer: 'Since you do not say when or set a limit, I do not know (and nor do you) what you mean by saying that you will phone "soon".' I might add more remarks such as, 'It may be the case that you do not want to commit yourself and so you engage in evasion. It may be that you have no intention of phoning and so you are saying that to cover your deception. It may be that you just want to put me off.'

Let us consider these answers.

Answer 1 specifies *a particular time*. So I know exactly where I stand. If they don't phone at three o'clock they have made a false prediction.

Answer 2 specifies *a limit* within which they will phone. If they do not phone within that limit, they too will have made a false prediction.

Answer 3 makes no specification and so leaves me confused. I do not know what to expect since they will not define 'soon'. So while they have apparently made a prediction with their sentence, they are not doing so. Their sentence can be neither fulfilled nor unfulfilled. It therefore cannot have the status of a prediction, or even of a claim at all. I must take my business elsewhere. I cannot do business in view of such prevarication.

What is very interesting is that adventists provide examples of each of these.

Case 1 Precise date:

Some adventists predicted that 1844 would be the end of all things. Other adventists foretold that the end would be in 1925, and there have been many other similar claims with a date specified.

Case 2 Date within a limited time span.

'Within the life time of those assembled here.'

Case 3 Refusal to specify either a date or a limit.

The principle is 'We do not set times.' This entails, 'Nor do we set limits'. The result is that they cannot and will not make any prediction about the time of the Advent. At the same time they just say that it will be 'soon'. The outcome of this is that 'soon' becomes a meaningless term.

Eschatology

Key Words

Sentence: words connected to form a grammatically complete expression of a single thought

Statement: a sentence making an assertion or claim

Cognitive: of sentences: making a claim, an assertion

Non-cognitive: of sentences: not making a claim.

Necessary: of logical connection, of implication: one statement entails the other,
      of statements: cannot be otherwise than true or false

Falsify: to show to be false

Falsification: the process of showing to be false

Verify: to show to be true

Verification: the process of showing to be true

Hortatory: giving warning, encouragement, exhortation; advisory

Empirical: based on observation, experiment, observation

Eschatological: having to do with the end

Entail: involve logically

Imply: involve logically

Chart

Sentences are either		
Cognitive	or	**Non-cognitive**
Inform		Advise
State fact		Warn
Assert		Exhort
Make claim		Admonish
		Command
		Question
Can be true or false		Cannot be true or false
Examples		
Jesus is coming again		Jesus is coming again soon (unspecifiable)
Jesus is coming again before 2050		We can't know when
Jesus is coming again within 20 years		No limit can be set

Eschatology
Confessional Statements

Traditional eschatology makes a more or less elaborate scheme of such 'last events'. It finds expression on different levels of complexity, some in very restrained statements. Others are extremely prolix. Here are some examples.

The **Apostles Creed states modestly**

He ascended into heaven from which he shall come to judge the living and the dead. I believe in the resurrection of the dead and the life everlasting.

The Nicene Creed

I look for the resurrection of the dead, and the life of the world to come. Amen

The Thirty-nine Articles

4. Of the Resurrection of Christ

Christ did truly rise again from death, and took again his body, with flesh, bones, and all things appertaining to the perfection of Man's nature; wherewith he ascended into Heaven, and there sitteth, until he return to judge all Men at the last day.

The Westminster Confession

Chapter 32. Of the State of Man After Death, and of the Resurrection of the Dead.

32.1. The bodies of men, after death, return to dust, and see corruption; but their souls (which neither die nor sleep), having an immortal subsistence, immediately return to God who gave them. The souls of the righteous, being then made perfect in holiness, are received into the highest heavens, where they behold the face of God in light and glory, waiting for the full redemption of their bodies; and the souls of the wicked are cast into hell, where they remain in torments and utter darkness, reserved to the judgement of the great day. Besides these two places for souls separated from their bodies, the Scripture acknowledges none.

32.2. At the last day, such as are found alive shall not die, but be changed: and all the dead shall be raised up with the self-same bodies, and none other, although with different qualities, which shall be united again to their souls forever.

32.3. The bodies of the unjust shall, by the power of Christ, be raised to dishonour; the bodies of the just, by his Spirit, unto honour, and be made conformable to his own glorious body.

Chapter 33. Of the Last Judgement.

33.1. God has appointed a day, wherein he will judge the world in righteousness by Jesus Christ, to whom all power and judgement is given of the Father. In which day, not only the apostate angels shall be judged; but likewise all persons, that have lived upon earth, shall appear before the tribunal of Christ, to give an account of their thoughts, words, and deeds; and to receive according to what they have done in the body, whether good or evil.

33.2. The end of God's appointing this day, is for the manifestation of the glory of his mercy in the eternal salvation of the elect; and of his justice in the damnation of the reprobate, who are wicked and disobedient. For then shall the righteous go into everlasting life, and receive that fullness of joy and refreshing which shall come from the presence of the Lord: but the wicked, who know not God, and obey not the gospel of Jesus Christ, shall be cast into eternal torments, and punished with everlasting destruction from the presence of the Lord, and from the glory of his power.

33.3. As Christ would have us to be certainly persuaded that there shall be a day of judgement, both to deter all men from sin, and for the greater consolation of the godly in their adversity: so will he have that day unknown to men, that they may shake off all carnal security, and be always watchful, because they know not at what hour the Lord will come; and may be ever prepared to say, Come, Lord Jesus, come quickly. Amen.

Eschatology

'The Fundamental Beliefs of Seventh-day Adventists'

A very elaborate statement, 742 words in all, is to be found here (*Year Book 2009, pp, 7-8.*), *under the headings:*
24. Christ's Ministry in the Heavenly Sanctuary
25. Second Coming of Christ
26. Death and Resurrection
27. Millennium and the End of Sin
28. New Earth

Key Terms

Eschatology

is the doctrine of the last (things). Eschatology has to do with the coming to an end; achieving a purpose, realising a goal, a *telos*. The nature of a thing is to be seen with reference to the end. End gives meaning and significance to all that precedes. The end explains the beginning and the continued existence of a thing. Hence the importance of the Christian virtue of **hope**, an orientation towards the future which gives meaning to the present. The present faith, the basis of Christian living, anticipates the fulfilment of the communion with God that under the limiting conditions of the present is now hampered and restricted.

End

The word *end* has two meanings quite distinct from each other. (1) It can mean 'termination', *finis*. Time passes and a process runs its course and proceeds no more. A thing lasts for so long and then is no more. A person dies and that is the end of life for her. Nothing is more final than the end which death brings. Such finality occurs with the passage of time. It is a terminus, pure and simple, whether any purpose is achieved or not. So 'end' here means *finis*, cessation, non-continuance, perhaps non-existence. (2) 'End' can also mean 'purpose,' 'goal,' 'objective'. So we ask, 'What is the end you have in view for this undertaking? You make a decision and then someone asks you, 'Do you realise what end the carrying out of this decision will achieve?' To the extent that we act with purposes in mind, we can speak of 'end' in this context and with this meaning. This use involves purposive action, conscious decision. It might even entail aspiration. An end is achieved when a subject acts with a goal in view, or with a goal implicit.

Ends may be relative or absolute. That one robin meets its end does not mean that the species meets its end. But that a language dies means that it is finally extinct and can be no more. So

Eschatology

we may qualify the term 'end' and speak of an ultimate end. We can envisage, for example, the absolute end of the universe. And of course some purposes are much more important then others. So there may be a personal 'end' of the utmost significance for the individual person. Religions are well aware of this. So are theologians. For example in the following quotation the notion of finality, and hence of end, is linked to that of decision, something taking place in the present:

> '. . . this necessity of decision constitutes the essential part of human nature. . . . If men are standing in the crisis of decision and if precisely this crisis is the essential characteristic of their humanity, then every hour is the last hour . . . [Jesus' conviction is] that even in the present man stands in the crisis of decision, that the present is for him the last hour.'[1]

The term 'end' or *eschaton* may also be used combining the two meanings we have just noted. Then it signifies that at the temporal *finis* of all things known to us, an ultimate purpose, a *telos*, will be achieved. That is the theme of traditional eschatology, to which the position expressed in the quotation above stands in contrast. *Eschaton* is the Greek word meaning 'end'. It has a wide reference to the events of the end-time. Discussion of these events is then called 'eschatology,' the doctrine of the end-time. Sometimes the theme is called 'the doctrine of the last things', a rather dull expression.

Advent

'Advent' means 'coming'. **'Second Advent'** means the return, the coming again of Jesus in glory to the world, to which he once before came in humility. The Greek term *parousia* has the same meaning, so that the terms are interchangeable.

adventist, Adventist

The term adventist (small initial letter) has general reference to all believers in the return; the coming of the Christ, called by Christians by agreement, the 'Second Advent'. It is a belief held

---

1 Rudolph Bultmann, *Jesus and the Word*, pp. 52, 56.

by most Christian confessions. So these are all adventists. However there are other means of expressing the conviction. One body of Christians uses the term in the name of their congregation, and so an initial capital letter is used, Adventist. These are the Seventh-day Adventists. The Hebrew also has long awaited and awaits the decisive coming of the Messiah. (Christ means Messiah.) In apocalyptic writings the Christ is awaited eagerly to bring in the New Age soon and to put an end to the present era of suffering.

There are two ways of expressing this hope. One is to express it with no reference to time by simply confessing, 'Christ is coming again', 'The Christ will come.' A second way is to stress the urgency implicit in the belief by adding a temporal reference, 'The coming is soon, is near, will be speedy.' Sometimes a specific period of time is expressed, Sometimes the time is left undefined, The coming will simply be soon, not within a limit nor after so many years, nor following so many predicted events. Apocalyptists, both Jewish and Christian think of the coming as near.

Kerygma means 'proclamation', 'preaching'. So it refers either to the **act** of proclaiming or to the **content** of the proclamation. Not that these are exclusive, for in the act of hearing (or reading) the proclamation you are made aware of the content, and thereby are influenced by it. The herald (*kerux*) is important, both in his act of announcing what he has to say and also because of the content of what he heralds.

The term is used specifically to refer to the proclamation of the word about Jesus of Nazareth. In existentialist eschatology it is the word that produces the crisis that is the essence of faith. So in this context gospel and *kerygma* come to be synonyms.

The ancient *kerygma*, as summarized[1] from Peter's speeches in *Acts* announces the following:

1 The Age of Fulfilment has dawned, the 'latter days' foretold by the prophets.

---

1 C. H. Dodd, *The Apostolic Preaching and its Developments*, pp. 21-23, 17.

2 This has taken place through the birth, life, ministry and death of Jesus Christ.

3 By virtue of the resurrection, Jesus has been exalted at the right hand of God as Messianic head of the new Israel.

4 The Holy Spirit in the church is the sign of Christ's present power and glory.

5 The Messianic Age will reach its consummation in the return of Christ.

6 An appeal is made for repentance with the offer of forgiveness, the Holy Spirit, and salvation.

The content is similar when reconstructed from the Pauline writings:

1. The prophecies are fulfilled and the New Age is inaugurated by the coming of Christ.
2. He was born of the seed of David.
3. He died according to the Scriptures, to deliver us out of the present evil age.
4. He was buried.
5. He rose on the third day according to the Scripture.
6. He is exalted to the right hand of God, as Son of God and Lord of quick and dead.
7. He will come again as Judge and Saviour of men.

It is through the act of proclamation of the Word about Jesus that Christian faith comes into being in the experience of the hearer. The Word is a living thing, not a dogma.

The *kerygma* is clearly eschatological. It announces the hope that Jesus will return as Lord and Judge.

Resurrection

Resurrection has two senses: the literal use, the action of being brought to life after dying and the analogical use, the transition from unfaith to faith. This transition is often described as the transition from death to life, even to 'eternal life' in the *Gospel of John* and in Pauline writings.

In the theology of Word and *Kerygma*, the terms 'resurrection' and 'resurrection life' are used of the understanding, of the faith that the proclamation brings to the believer. That understanding is 'eschatological'.

Myth

In our context there are two basic meanings: (1) an ancient world view and its elements, a cosmology of a three-storied universe: flat earth, heaven above, hell beneath. This is the framework for ascension from a point on a flat earth to a heaven above the earth. (2) purported statements about the activity and acts of supernatural beings as the cause of effects within the cosmos. e.g. God causing the earth to open, punishing the wrong doers by instant death. Satan as a transcendent evil being causing violence in the heavens and death and havoc on the earth.

The content of myth is presented in the form of narrative, e.g. Angels appear and speak to humans or cause fire to the wicked.

History

The English word has two distinct meanings; what happened, and what is reported or written about what happened. So the word means either an event or series of events, or the account that records and interprets events, or both. Caesar's crossing the Rubicon is an event. The account given of the event is an interpreted report. The production of an account is, of course, an event.

In German there are two words **Historie** and **Geschichte**. Some theologians differentiate between them, applying *Historie* to the event or series of events, what happened, and *Geschichte* to one's experience or understanding of the event or series of events. This latter is an existential use of the term.

DISCUSSION QUESTIONS
Chapter 9

(1) The word 'soon' and its synonyms have temporal reference and so only have meaning when that temporal reference is made clear. Discuss in ordinary secular common-garden terms, giving your own examples.

(2) State clearly the meaning of the phrase cognitively meaningful. Give examples of cognitively meaningful sentences. In contrast find and discuss examples of cognitively meaningless sentences.

(3) Distinguish and give examples of sentences that are exclamatory, emotive, hortatory. Consult the chart on page 67.

(4) Relate your responses to these questions to the claim that the Advent is imminent.

10

THE END AFTER THE END

The term eschatology is a comprehensive one. We can separate out two meanings. As generally understood, it has reference to the events that bring the present world to its end. The terms 'end time', 'last things' refer to the final events that bring human history to its close. These 'last things' have to do with the cosmos as we know it, to life as we have lived it, to history as it comes to its terminus. It is about the end of our world. The terms have reference to the teaching about those final events that bring human history to a close. Different believers and their communities have their own interpretations as to what will then take place. Some map out in great detail the series of events which, when they have run their course, will introduce a 'new heavens and a new earth'.

But what is this end, this *eschaton*? It is the watershed between two different orders of existence. This 'end' introduces a beginning, the beginning of life renewed, 'eternal' life. We now ask how we can conceive the nature of this new existence. What options are there for us to contemplate? In addition to speaking of the events that lead to a new age and of our transition to it, we now think about the kind of existence there may be in the new age. One theme talks of bringing the world to its end. The other attempts to produce a description of the nature of the new age and personal existence within it.

First, as in what has preceded, we have engaged in what is sometimes called 'pareschatology'. This is an explanatory description of the belief in the series of events leading to the 'end' of human history and the establishment of the 'new heavens and the new earth'. Some Christian communities elaborate such descriptions in great detail, drawing largely on the apocalyptic visions of the New Testament.

Second and now, we discuss the issues involved as we pose questions about the existence after the 'end'.

The end of human life is death. None escape.

> Death lays his icy hand on kings:
> Sceptre and crown
> Must tumble down,
> And in the dust be equal made
> With the poor crooked scythe and spade.
> James Shirley

The quest thus becomes one with the universal problem concerning life after death. When we ask whether there is life after the individual death and when we ask whether there is life after the end of all human life, after the end of the world, the answer we give will address both questions.

What becomes clearer as we examine this second theme is that it has puzzled human beings for millennia. Both secular philosophers and committed believers have spent great efforts in engaging in the attempt to provide answers.

To this common problem Christians have, in the main, given two different answers. The first is that after death, there will be resurrection, and after resurrection there will be, for the righteous, continuing life. This renewal of life will be in the body. It will be a physical existence.

The second answer, inherited from Plato and predominant for many centuries in Christian churches, was that the human person is constituted by an immortal soul. At death the soul, that 'real person' will be freed from the body within which it has had its confining house, its sojourn during earthly days. It will then be free and unrestricted.

Both approaches bring us to the point where we have to consider what it means to claim that there is an eternal life beyond this existence. Pareschatology brings us to the point of departure, so to speak, and in thousands of funeral and memorial services it is often vaguely and sentimentally proffered that all is well and we are offered the contemplation of eternal life as a most desirable state. Those who mourn can therefore take comfort. But what is the nature of this most desirable state?

The difficult task is to conceive it with any degree of certainty and satisfaction. It is not possible within the limits of this writing to engage in an extended theological or philosophical discussion of the issues here involved. That is for another writing: to discuss the theme of death, survival, immortality and the identity of the human person. What we can do here is to ask whether we can form some constructive ideas concerning what kind such post mortem life will be? How far shall we conceive it on an analogy with the life we now know and still be able to provide a reasonable account.

Will we learn from relations of a social kind with other surviving creatures? Will we engage in progressive learning? As we progress through the years shall we develop into persons we would not otherwise have been? For, after all, personality is attained, developed, and changed through experience and learning. In our short span of earthly life, we developed into different persons than we were when we approached and then emerged from adolescence. But everlasting life is a very, very, very long time and provides opportunities for continuous development and so to became quite different in competence, in interest, in social ability, in contemplative capacity and so on, and so on and so on.

That sounds rather different from the minimal and often sentimental things we hear about being without tears, there being no night in the realms 'above', about having no pain and distress, about playing harps and singing endless paeans of praise. Those and other activities of incredible diversity would produce great variety of personality and social unity at any given time and great variety over time, assuming time and space of course. Will there be varying degrees of the different capacities we shall possess? Will different persons be possessed of differing degrees of intelligence and different capacities for development as they develop in different directions?

Unless we can give some answers to these questions we would have to leave the idea of eternal life without content and vague. That might satisfy the uninquiring. It is not an adequate basis for a meaningful hope. But once we begin to contemplate the idea of 'everlasting' and attempt to give content to the concept of eternity and endless life, it is hardly satisfying to be told that it's all in God's wise hands and that it will be good, even if we can form no idea about that good thing it will be.

A crucial issue concerns how we shall think of the relation between the person who dies and the person who survives. In what sense can one be thought of as the same person if transformed and readied for life in a new world, even in a different space and time than the one we now know. We can give reasons why the person who survives into the eternal world should be the same person as the one who died in this world. But the challenge then is to provide a reasonable account of what that identity involves. Even if opinions differ as to what it means to be the same person over time in this present world we come to agreement when we have to make a judgement about a particular person. Indeed we are always doing so in our practical social living. The questions are, 'What constitutes Mary the same person now that she was twenty years ago?' 'What conditions must be fulfilled if we are to decide that Mr. X is the same person as the Mr. X we knew fifty years ago?'

But a further account is needed to indicate what it would mean for us to be able to say that this one is the same person in two different worlds, with death in between the transition from the one to the other? Only if a satisfactory account can be given may we speak of 'survival'. The Christian belief in resurrection and immortality demands such elucidation. What is involved for there to be continuity of the person is consciousness, an environment, the ability to will and to act, space and objects in space, as suggested in the following statement.

For continued personal identity would seem to require the continuation of a finite consciousness, aware of an environment from a particular perspective within it, and able to exercise volition in relating to that environment. The very notion of an environment seems to presuppose space, filled with a variety of objects, and interaction with that environment seems to presuppose that we are embodied as one of the space-filling objects.[1]

The difficulty is how we are to think of these conditions existing in a cosmos beyond our experience and initiated by God who ensures such continuity of consciousness.

So we may well be reticent i.e. understandably agnostic in making pronouncements about the future life. Paul's words stand as exemplary of this attitude: 'Eye hath not seen nor ear heard, nor hath it entered into the heart of man the things that God hath prepared for those that love him' (*I Corinthians* 2:9). We note also his hesitation about the kind of body that we might possibly have. He observed. 'There is a physical body and there is a spiritual body.' But he is prepared to leave it with that non-committal observation, simply insisting that there will be an appropriate heavenly body for the new existence. That God will provide. (*I Corinthians* 15: 35-50). He trusts that all will be well. But he makes no effort to assert the identity of the heavenly person with the earthly one. He seems to take it for granted. On another occasion he considered it most desirable to abandon this earthly existence for the heavenly one. 'For I am in a strait betwixt two, having a desire to depart, and to be with Christ; which is far better' (*Philippians* 1:23). There is no suggestion of fear or apprehension, but only of desire. Nor is there any attempt to elaborate.

The Post Mortem State: Resurrection as Replication

Death marks the end of this embodied existence. Renewal of life marks the beginning of a new existence. How shall the renewed person begin that renewed life? Christian believers have insisted

---

1   John Hick, *Death and Eternal Life*. London: Collins, 1976, p. 276.

that any renewal of life beyond death will be the result of God's recreation of the dead. Christian creeds have always included the clause about the final resurrection. Is it possible to produce some clarity as to what this might mean? How shall we think about it? How can we conceive the process and the outcome?

Augustine confronted the problem. But his answer, both sincere and hopeful, is hardly available for us. He wrote:

'the dust of bodies long dead shall return with incomprehensible facility and swiftness to those members that are now to live endlessly.'[1]

---

1 *The City of God*, XXII, 20.

Augustine's statement recognizes the difficulties, but holds that the power of the Creator will overcome them. He cites specific cases: bodies eaten by wild beasts, by cannibals, bodies that have disintegrated. However the death took place God can recall the flesh that originally constituted the body. In the case of those who has starved and so lost flesh, that flesh will be restored. Even if the original flesh has entirely disintegrated, God can restore it. 'His own flesh ... which he lost by famine, shall be restored to him by Him who can recover even what has evaporated.' And 'though it had been absolutely annihilated, so that no part of its substance remained in any secret spot of nature, the Almighty could restore it by such means as He saw fit.' The flesh of bodies eaten by cannibals, will be restored to the man in whom it first began to be human flesh!

But the restored body will not be weak or diseased. It will be the body at its best or what would have been its best had it developed. That body will enjoy 'the beauty that arises from preserving symmetry and proportion of all its members.' All deformity and ugliness will be removed from the earthly body. The one who is resurrected will rise 'with the precise stature he had when he departed this life', The living body, even if it 'ceased to be an entity in any particular place', the 'power of the Almighty Creator' will reassemble. There will be 'no deformity, no infirmity, no languor, no corruption' as the identical particles are recreated. Not a hair of its head will perish. The exact same body will be restored, even if no particles remain.

We are left with the decisive question. Grant that God can gather, recreate and reform flesh particles, making a body out of nothing, that body cannot be said, especially if its former deformities and weaknesses have been removed from it, to be the same body as the one which died. Flesh newly created cannot be the same flesh as the flesh that once was and that is no more! Of the body that was, Augustine is convinced 'God Almighty can recall it and make "it" the one that is to be.' That is not beyond the capacity of the Creator.

We know that there is no permanence, even fixity, to the physical body. No particle of my past body is now in my present body. So if we talk of having the 'same body' over a period of time it cannot be in the sense of the identity of physical particles. In a few years time every particle of my present physical body will be replaced. Physically I am being constantly reconstituted.

There is however a continuity between my earlier body and my present body. It is this continuity that ceases at death. So with the dissolution of the particles the old body ceases to be. The confession that the resurrected person is the same person as the one who died must recognise that there is a gap between the body that was and the reconstituted person. It is this that puzzled Paul with his contrast between physical and spiritual bodies. He does not solve but simply states his problem: With what body do they come? Cf. *I Corinthians* 15:35-50.

The hope of the Christian is that God will bring about the new age by reconstituting the persons who have perished. But what of the bodily materials that have perished? Can an identical person be constituted without the continuity of the physical body? A further criterion for one to be the same person at time 2 that she was at time 1 is that she have the same memories. Would possession of the same memories by itself suffice to identify the person at the *eschaton*?

Augustine was prepared to go to such lengths because he was convinced that to be the same person one had to have the identical body at different times.

We are left with the question whether in the celestial sphere there can be an identical person without the bodily continuity we require in our terrestrial investigations. What is clear is that if there is to be a resurrection of the body, that resurrection body will have to be created anew. However the 'replicated' heavenly person will have restored memories in that new body. The process of continuing post-mortem creation has there its beginning. The purpose of the original creation has reached its final but continuing stage.

This accords with Paul's distinction between different kinds of body and his nsistence on God's initiative. *I Corinthians* 15:38, 40, 44.

For more extended discussion see my *Death, Immortality and Resurrection*, II. 3.

This would initially be a first person identification. I would have memories I recognise as having had before. A third person recognition that I am the same person he once knew would depend on that person having a previous knowledge of at least some of the other's memory and becoming acquainted with them again at the later time.

At resurrection there is no bodily connection to the earthly physical body. The heavenly body is not continuous with that previous body, for after death it has disintegrated. However, Christian belief in resurrection to life beyond death requires that the person resurrected be the same person as the one who lived previously. So we need a satisfactory idea of identity that we can reasonably apply to the eschatological situation. Since we are considering a unique situation involving the transcendent God and his activity, it is desirable that we find a suitable way of employing the idea of 'same person' to that eschatological situation. Within our present existence we have a suitable concept of personal identity. Does the idea of 'replica' provide a suitable concept of personal identity to fit the eschatological state?

We then will say that the later person is a 'replica' of the former. As a 'replica', the person post mortem is the 'same person' as the earthly person' means that the heavenly person is a 'replica' of the earthly. The idea of replication enables us to imagine various situations which may be taken as analogies to the idea of resurrection. When we employ that idea we shall give meaning to the new and astonishing situation in which a person is identical between two realms of existence. We may then understand that a certain set of circumstances (however they come to be or are brought about) would fulfil the appropriate conditions so that we would decide that Mary is the same person as the one who died and whose remains exist no more.

Let's take an analogy from situations we can imagine. One scenario, having appeared in science fiction, has found its place in philosophical discussion and now in theology. We imagine someone disappearing from one place and someone exactly similar appearing in another. For example:

Edward disappears from Nottingham and someone exactly similar appears in Vancouver.

William disappears from Nottingham and someone exactly similar appears on Mars.

Harry disappears from Nottingham, and someone exactly similar appears in a heavenly sphere, the New Jerusalem.

In each of these cases we can imagine two different circumstances. In the one case there is no trace of the original physical body. So no body remains in Nottingham. In the other cases the body has died, and so physical elements remain in Nottingham. But now there is no further trace of the original physical body. We then ask in each of the six cases how, if it is possible at all, we might speak of personal identity.

Consider the idea of replica. We call the exactly similar entity a replica, provided that that entity has been fashioned by reference to the original. The term 'replica' means something very similar, if not exactly similar. We might, if we do not use the term strictly, speak of a poor replica, a botched attempt at replication. Moreover, there can be more than one such entity. Sometimes the term might even denote a forgery, since the best kind of forgery is indistinguishable from the original. The term has reference to something that is qualitatively similar to the original, from which it has been derived. The original is the model from which the replica has been copied. So hundred dollar bills and twenty pound notes are in this sense replicas of an original. And the less they are in value the more they are in quantity. So we may, if we choose, qualify the term 'replica' which we then should indicate with quotation marks, to mean an object qualitatively the same as the original. Given this qualification the object referred to by the term (now in inverted commas) can only be one object, a singular item. It cannot be quantitatively identical with the original (and would not be, even on Augustine's terms). The original no longer exists.

In the case of resurrection, there is only one resurrected person. So we stipulate that the replicated entity is unique, i.e. there can only be one of these. The original has forever disappeared. We use the term of only one item, one person. We indicate this use by putting the term in quotes, as 'replica'.

So we have our analogy. Think of Edward in Vancouver. Think of William on Mars. Think of Harry in the New Jerusalem. Insist in each case that there be only one and you have a workable analogy. The heavenly 'replica' is unique and has all the essential qualities of the original, is qualitatively identical in those essential identifying properties. Mind you, we shall then have to go further and say what we think those essential identifying properties of personal identity over time in our ordinary experience are as we make application to the post-mortem situation.

There are two: (1) continuity of physical properties and (2) possession of the same memories. We identify someone we know by recalling and attributing their physical features to a particular person. But with the long passage of time such features undergo change. So recognising someone by this means my not be conclusive, may not even be possible. What would be decisive would be that we establish he and I have memories which only we two share. We shared a secret as children, a code word let's say, and we have both kept the secret.

For Edward and William, the new residents in Vancouver, and on Mars, identical memories will be sufficient if reference to physical features cannot be got. If it were available, exact similarity of such physical features would provide corroborative evidence. In terrestrial cases it would be the primary evidence of identity.

No doubt in each of these cases we have to decide whether we are going to say that the conditions fulfilled would allow us to apply the term 'identity' to the 'replica' If such situations came about there is no doubt that we would do so. In the resurrection case we would now be ready to say that the 'replica' is identical to the person who previously lived. The 'same person' has survived.[1]

What has taken place is that we shall be using old language for a situation we have never encountered, explaining the new associations with the familiar terms. We interpret the new phenomena by employing, duly modified, our understanding of the old.

In sum. In addressing the question, How might we show that the person so replicated at the *eschaton*, is identical with the former terrestrial person? We extend the same considerations by which we define personal identity now. We apply them with due qualification to the person replicated after death and in a new space. We revise the meaning of the terms 'identity', 'same person' so that they now have reference to situations we had not previously encountered, but which we can even now readily imagine.

God produces a 'replica'. We may elucidate the essential conviction that the resurrected person is the same person as the earthly person by employing the idea of 'replication'. But the 'how' of the creative act is beyond us. We can give no account of the divine action of resurrection. The believer has never claimed to be able to do so.

Limitless Transformation?

Reintroduced to new life in a new space, we shall immediately be transformed into new persons. But where we begin is not where we shall remain. For as persons we develop. A total transformation at resurrection would mean that we lose our identity with the person we were at death. We die without having attained to the persons we might have been. Since if we start where we were, where we have finished here, we must say that we are by no means perfected. I die as did Claudius, Hamlet's father, 'with all my imperfections on my head'. Where I finish, that is where I shall begin in the new earth! So my existence will be of two parts, the present and the future, or from the perspective of that future of the resurrected, the present

---

[1] D. Parfitt, *Reasons and Persons,* Oxford: University Press, 1984, p. 201: 'I ought to regard a replica as being about as good as ordinary survival.'

and the past: of memory, experience and anticipation. The great transition is from the one to the other.

But surely to be fit for heavenly existence we shall have to make some progress if we have not attained to holiness or perfection in this earthly life. Opportunity seems required to enable the resurrected one to make such progress, occasion for removing the imperfections we have brought with us. For the catholic this is provided by the teaching about purgatory.

The believer anticipates the post mortem future we are now contemplating as limitless by speaking of 'eternal' life. That means that in the new existence the past will become longer and longer. The theoretical possibility is that with everlasting life in prospect there will become an infinity of memories as limitless as there is an existence in infinite time.

In a few decades in this earthly existence I become a different person as I learn, experience and mature. Indeed, in this present life I may undergo several changes of personality. In eternity the capacities for change would be endless. The problem of memory then emerges and with it the problem of my continuing identity.[1]

---

1 For an exposition of this understanding cf. John Hick, *op. cit.*, pp. 409-412. Terence Penelhum observes that the identification is a decision rather than a discovery and then raises the question whether it warrants us to expect ourselves to be 'one of these post-mortem beings in the future.' *Survival and Disembodied Existence*. London: Routledge & Kegan Paul, 1980, pp. 100-102. But we observe that there must be features we discover before we are able to come to the decision that we are the same person as we were. It looks like a verbal point.

Discussion Questions
Chapter 10

(1) Is it important that the person who survives at the *eschaton* be the same person that lived and died on earth?

(2) How would I identify someone whom I once new decades ago as the same person whom I am now meeting? And she me?

(3) Consider the meaning of the term replica. Does the term, duly qualified, help us to understand the idea that we shall be personally identical in the resurrection to the person we were here on earth?

(4) How do you conceive the resurrected person as identical with the former terrestrial person, fit for celestial existence without some transformation?

(5) If raised the same person without that transformation, how shall that transformation take place. A kind of purgatory? Some kind of development? Taking time?

BIBLIOGRAPHY

Barrett, C. K. *The Gospel according to St John*. London: S. P. C. K, 1956.

Barth, Karl. *Church Dogmatics. Volume III, Part two*. Edinburgh: T. & T. Clark, 1960.

Brunner, Emil. *The Christian Doctrine of the Church, Faith, and the Consummation*. Dogmatics: Vol. III. pp. 425-444.

Bultmann, Rudolf. *Theology of the New Testament*. Translated by Kendrick Grobel. London: S. C. M. Press, Volume one. 1956. Volume two 1958.

Bultmann, Rudolf. (Hans Werner Bartsch (editor), Reginald H. Fuller, translator). 'New Testament and Mythology' in *Kerygma and Myth*, London: S. P. C .K., 1972.

Bultmann, Rudolf. *Jesus and the Word*. New York: Charles Scribner's Sons, 1958.

Conzelmann, Hans. *An Outline of the Theology of the New Testament*. Translated by John Bowden. London: S. C. M. Press, 1969.

Conzlemann, Hans. *The Theology of St. Luke*. New York: Harper and Row, 1961.

Cullmann, Oscar. *Salvation in History*. Translated by Sidney G. Sowers et al. New York: Harper & Row, 1967.

Dodd, C. H. *The Apostolic Preaching and its Developments*. London: Hodder and Stoughton, 1936 (1951); New York: Harper and Row, 1964.

Dodd, C. H. *The Parables of the Kingdom*. Glasgow: Collins, 1983.

Hefner, Philip. *Faith and the Vitalities of History*. New York: Harper and Row, 1966.

Hunter, A. M. *The Word and Words of Jesus*. London: S. C. M. Press, 1950.

Kähler, Martin. *The So-called Historical Jesus and the Historic Biblical Christ*. Translated by Carl E. Braaten. Philadelphia: Fortress Press, 1964. (Original German Edition, 1896).

Moltmann, Jürgen. *Theology of Hope*. Translated by James W. Leitch. London: S. C. M. Press, 1965.

Mowinckel, Sigmund. *He that Cometh*. Translated by G. W. Anderson. Oxford: Basil Blackwell, 1959.

Pannenberg, Wolfhart. *The Apostles Creed in the Light of Today's Questions*. London: S. C. M. Press, 1972.

Plato. B. Jowett (translator). *The Dialogues of Plato, Volume 1*. New York: Random House, 1937, pp. 450-451.

Quick, Oliver C. *Doctrines of the Creed*. London: Collins, 1968. p. 264.

Richardson, Alan. *Christian Apologetics*. London: S. C. M. Press, 1947.

Rowland, Christopher. *Christian Origins*. London: S. P. C. K., 1985.

Russell, D. S. *Apocalyptic Ancient and Modern*. London: S. C. M. Press, 1978.

Sanders, E. P. *Jesus and Judaism*. Philadelphia: Fortress Press, 1958.

Vick, Edward W. H. *Death, Immortality and Resurrection* (MS).

Vick, Edward W. H. *The Adventists' Dilemma*. Nottingham: Evening Publications, 2001.

Vick, Edward W. H. *History and Christian Faith*. Nottingham: Evening Publications, 2003.

ALSO FROM ENERGION PUBLICATIONS

... masterful contribution to a vexed and timely topic.

Lawrence T. Geraty, Ph.D.
President Emeritus
La Sierra University.

... informed, clear, and immensely helpful.

Richard Rice
Professor of Religion
Loma Linda University

More from Energion Publications

Personal Study
Finding My Way in Christianity	Herold Weiss	$16.99
Holy Smoke! Unholy Fire	Bob McKibben	$14.99
The Jesus Paradigm	David Alan Black	$17.99
When People Speak for God	Henry Neufeld	$17.99
The Sacred Journey	Chris Surber	$11.99

Christian Living
Faith in the Public Square	Robert D. Cornwall	$16.99
Grief: Finding the Candle of Light	Jody Neufeld	$8.99
Soup Kitchen for the Soul	Renee Crosby	$12.99
Crossing the Street	Robert LaRochelle	$16.99

Bible Study
Learning and Living Scripture	Lentz/Neufeld	$12.99
From Inspiration to Understanding	Edward W. H. Vick	$24.99
Luke: A Participatory Study Guide	Geoffrey Lentz	$8.99
Philippians: A Participatory Study Guide	Bruce Epperly	$9.99
Ephesians: A Participatory Study Guide	Robert D. Cornwall	$9.99

Theology
Creation in Scripture	Herold Weiss	$12.99
Creation: the Christian Doctrine	Edward W. H. Vick	$12.99
The Politics of Witness	Allan R. Bevere	$9.99
Ultimate Allegiance	Robert D. Cornwall	$9.99
History and Christian Faith	Edward W. H. Vick	$9.99
The Church Under the Cross	William Powell Tuck	$11.99
The Journey to the Undiscovered Country	William Powell Tuck	$9.99

Ministry
Clergy Table Talk	Kent Ira Groff	$9.99
Out of This World	Darren McClellan	$24.99

Generous Quantity Discounts Available
Dealer Inquiries Welcome
Energion Publications — P.O. Box 841
Gonzalez, FL_ 32560
Website: http://energionpubs.com
Phone: (850) 525-3916

www.ingramcontent.com/pod-product-compliance
Lightning Source LLC
LaVergne TN
LVHW011203080426
835508LV00007B/574